BREAKING THE CHAINS

ONE CHRISTIAN'S ACCOUNT OF WHY HE LEFT THE MORMON CHURCH

By Nathan Franson

PUBLISHED BY

COBB PUBLISHING

Cobb Publishing
704 E. Main St.
Charleston, AR 72933
https://CobbPublishing.com

Copyright © 2024 Nathan Franson
Design by Lee Snow

ISBN: 978-1-960858-47-4

Library of Congress Control Number: 2017950939
Version 2.0

All rights reserved by publisher. No part of this book may be reproduced in any form without express written permission from the publisher or its authorized representative.

Discover Other Titles
By Cobb Publishing
https://CobbPublishing.com

Dedicated to my wife Katy, who has been a rock during the process of writing this. Thank you for allowing me the long and often demanding hours buried in my office putting this together, and for your invaluable encouragement. I love you infinity.

CONTENTS

BREAKING THE CHAINS I
PREFACE VII
FOREWORD XI
HISTORY ACCORDING TO THE MORMON CHURCH 1
THE GODHEAD 19
HOW RELIABLE IS THE BOOK OF MORMON? 35
OFFICES AND PRIESTHOODS 53
ESCHATOLOGY 75
LDS PROPHECIES 87
THE BOOK OF ABRAHAM AND THE SENSEN PAPYRI 101
THE PLAN OF SALVATION 117
AFTERWORD 137

PREFACE

Seldom is anyone led out of a denomination or religious affiliation quickly and without contemplation. Most of the time it involves a process in which one begins to question certain aspects, arriving at a conclusion and eventually leading to a final decision. It was no different for me. As a youth growing up in Salt Lake City, Utah I was excited to be part of something my mother and those adults surrounding me encouraged. I was baptized at the age of eight years old. I became a Deacon at the age of twelve and received the Aaronic Priesthood. "Passing the Sacrament" (the equivalent of assisting on the Lord's table) was an honor. Every first Sunday of the month was the tradition of "Fast Sunday" in which we would go without two meals that day. It was also the worship service in which members had the opportunity to stand in front of the congregation and "bare their testimony," or give an account of what they were thankful for and what God had done in their lives. I was baptized for the dead. Eventually I had the privilege of baptizing my younger brother. Social gatherings were a regular occurrence. It was a time of anticipating the age when we would eventually be able to participate in the two-year mission, unknown where we would go until assigned by Church headquarters. This was life growing up and it was the life I knew as normal. Then things began to change.

Questions I had about different subjects and topics were answered with inconclusive, ambiguous, or simply unsatisfying replies. Some of it was kept concealed, as I did not understand why others were not questioning the same matters or just accepted a vague response from teachers and the Bishop. Soon the doubt set in as the more I studied and sought clarification the more I felt disconnected. Finally, about the age of twenty years old, I decided it was time to walk away. Through the course of events I lost the friendships of some, while simply falling out of touch with others. Several people attempted to lure me back. There was never an angry criticism by anyone, nor was there a hostile attitude, at least to me. They simply stopped communicating. When

BREAKING THE CHAINS

I first started questioning my LDS faith I was approximately eighteen years old and ready to graduate high school.

My mother took it the hardest. She questioned herself as to why she did not do an adequate job raising me. Our discussions would often result in arguments. Being young and inexperienced and trying to reason a subject as delicate as this was, my approach probably could have been better. However, I knew Mormonism would no longer be a part of my life. There were spurts after leaving where I was either non-religious altogether or grasping for some form of Bible understanding of which to make sense.

For several years I held on to animosity towards the Mormon faith. In my mind if that was not the true church then nothing could be, which is a common response from those who have left. Several years passed before I was comfortable to discuss my background without allowing emotions to direct the conversation. As a result I studied with someone who had me read the book of Acts. It led me to be baptized into Christ and added to His church (Acts 2:38, 47).

This book represents years of information taken from my own experiences living as a member of the Church of Jesus Christ of Latter Day Saints in addition to hours of research. The purpose of its content is two-fold. One is to assist those seeking to know more about the Mormon Church. It is also for those members of the LDS faith who are curious why I would leave or are questioning it themselves, seeking deeper answers or explanations. Whatever the case, the Bible is maintained as the final and respected standard of authority. Some of the material presented may challenge the beliefs of those who read it. Others may disagree with it, which is fine. It is never wrong to stand for what we believe is the truth, but it is equally important to weigh the evidence. Be honest, sincere and open when pursuing any investigation before arriving at a conclusion. The key is to define terms. While some may appear to be the same as how the Bible words it on the surface, the definition may be considerably different.

For anyone who may be searching for answers or even doubting, know you are not alone. I felt isolated in my investigation, but realized there are others who are going through the same. It can be difficult, but necessary when your eternal life is on the line. Trust the Bible. Find someone who

PREFACE

is a crutch on which to lean. It can be a challenging and often perilous transition but you can get through it. My hope with this book is it is able to offer insight and be a valuable resource for the honest student.

Nathan Franson

FOREWORD

Keith A. Mosher, Sr. D.Min.

This book, on the backgrounds of Mormonism, is the result of a painful and difficult journey from a childhood religion to the adult convictions that the faith once held by the author was one that did not consist of truth. I have known Nathan Franson for about fifteen years as a true friend, former student of mine at the Memphis School of Preaching in Memphis, Tennessee, and a fellow Christian dedicated to the restoration of New Testament Christianity. In fact, he and his wife, Katy, honored me by giving their son, Micah, my first name as his middle name. However, when Nathan asked me to write the forward to this expose, I was somewhat apprehensive. The reason for my edginess follows.

When anyone leaves a religion, even one that is man-made, many of that person's friends and family members are heart-broken or even angry. Why? Because it is commonly taught that "one religion is as good as another" and that "everyone just needs to be sincere in what he believes." For Nathan, however, truth became more important than family and friends, especially after he was introduced to the words of Jesus that: "He that loveth father or mother more than me is not worthy of me: and he that loveth son or daughter more than me is not worthy of me" (Mat. 10:37). Nathan eventually studied all of Jesus' words found in the New Testament and truth was learned. Nathan then knew that he could no longer stay in Mormonism regardless of family connections and regardless of friendships. He thus wrote this book, not to "put down" anyone, but to encourage anyone who reads this material to search for Bible truth and not to be discouraged by anyone in the effort.

The founder of Mormonism, Joseph Smith, was, per their claims, illiterate, and one would be led to ask how Smith could have written

XI

BREAKING THE CHAINS

the book of Mormon. It seems Smith's friend, Sidney Rigdon (a former member of the church of Christ) had helped. It is truly ironic that Nathan Franson has written this book having left Mormonism and having become a member of the church of Christ one can read about in the New Testament.

God will always bless all who seek truth: "If any man will do his will, he shall know of the doctrine, whether it be of God, or whether I speak of myself" (John 7:17). May all who read brother Franson's material keep the latter verse in mind as they discover the deceptions, errors, and falsehoods, uncovered here, about the Church of Christ of Latter Day Saints.

Dean of Academics and Student Life
Memphis School of Preaching

1

HISTORY ACCORDING TO THE MORMON CHURCH

Beginning at a very young age we were saturated with Mormon history. Along with my friends, I was encouraged by my teachers to study the Articles of Faith along with the Book of Mormon. We saw it as an exciting time to be able to mature as faithful followers. By the time I was a teenager I was proud I could recite vividly how Joseph Smith started the Church of Jesus Christ of Latter Day Saints.

Before examining how Joseph Smith claims the Mormon Church began, it would benefit the unfamiliar reader to understand how favored Joseph Smith is to them. This may help in realizing why so many would follow his plan.

John Taylor, a member of the Council of the Twelve Apostles, writes,

> Joseph Smith, the Prophet and Seer of the Lord, has done more, save Jesus only, for the salvation of men in this world, than any other man that ever lived in it. In the short space of twenty years, he has brought forth the Book of Mormon, which he translated by the gift and power of God, and has been the means of publishing it on two continents; has sent the fullness of the everlasting gospel, which it contained, to the four quarters of the earth; has brought forth the revelations and commandments which compose this book of Doctrine and Covenants, and many other wise documents and instructions for the

benefit of the children of men; gathered many thousands of the Latter-day Saints, founded a great city, and left a fame and name that cannon be slain. He lived great, and he died great in the eyes of God and his people... (Doctrine & Covenants 135:3)

Joseph Fielding Smith, the great, great nephew of Joseph Smith wrote, "Mormonism, as it is called, must stand or fall on the story of Joseph Smith. He was either a prophet of God, divinely called, properly appointed and commissioned, or he was one of the biggest frauds this world has ever seen. There is no middle ground." (J. F. Smith)

Joseph Smith confidently stated,

Come on! ye prosecutors! ye false swearers! All hell, boil over! Ye burning mountains, roll down your lava! for I will come out on top at last. I have more to boast of than ever any man had. I am the only man that has ever been able to keep a whole church together since the days of Adam. A large majority of the whole have stood by me. Neither Paul, John, Peter, nor Jesus ever did it. I boast that no man ever did such a work as I. The followers of Jesus ran away from Him; but the Latter-day Saints never ran away from me yet...

(J. Smith, History of the Church)

It is dangerous and irresponsible to put so much confidence in a man without testing him. Even the apostles urged people to not just take their word for it. Paul writes, "Prove all things; hold fast that which is good." (1 Thes. 5:21) Luke writes concerning Paul and Silas' assessment of the Bereans, "These were more noble than those in Thessalonica, in that they received the word with all readiness of mind, and searched the scriptures daily, whether those things were so." (Act 17:11) John writes, "Beloved, believe not every spirit, but try the spirits whether they are of God: because many false prophets are gone out into the world." (1 Joh 4:1)

HISTORY ACCORDING TO THE MORMON CHURCH
JOSEPH SMITH AND HIS FIRST VISION ACCOUNT

The Mormon Church teaches what they call "The Great Apostasy." It is the belief that after the death of Christ and His apostles, man wiped His church and doctrine from the earth. They contend after Christ and His apostles had died, men corrupted the principles of the gospel of Christ and made unauthorized changes in Church organization and priesthood ordinances.

The Doctrine and Covenants and Church History Seminar Teacher Manual reads,

> Jesus Christ established His Church during His ministry on the earth. "The Apostles, after the Ascension of Christ, continued to exercise the keys He left with them. But because of disobedience and loss of faith by the members, the Apostles died without the keys being passed on to successors. We call that tragic episode 'the Apostasy.'" Because of this widespread apostasy, the Lord took the priesthood authority away from the people. Understanding the Great Apostasy helps us better understand the need for the Restoration of the gospel of Jesus Christ in the latter days... The Great Apostasy occurred during the centuries following the Lord's mortal ministry...Apostasy occurs when people turn away from the true doctrine of the gospel and reject the Lord's authorized servants...Periods of general apostasy have occurred throughout the history of the world. One example is the Great Apostasy, which occurred after the Savior established His Church (see 2 Thessalonians 2:1–3). Following the deaths of the Savior's Apostles, the principles of the gospel were corrupted and unauthorized changes were made in Church organization and to priesthood ordinances.
>
> (Seminaries and Institutes of Religion Curriculum Services 8-10)

As a result, Joseph Smith claimed God the Father and Jesus the Son in heavenly but fleshly tangible forms visited him and divinely revealed to him how to "restore" the true church. In essence, the entire premise of Mormonism rests on this professed testimony of a teenager.

He wrote,

> Some time in the second year after our removal to Manchester [New York], there was in the place where we lived an unusual excitement on the subject of religion. It commenced with the Methodists, but soon became general among all the sects in that region of the country…great multitudes united themselves to the different religious parties, which created no small stir and division among the people…the great zeal manifested by the respective clergy, who were active in getting up and promoting this extraordinary scene of religious feeling, in order to have everybody converted, as they were pleased to call it, let them join what sect they pleased…I was at this time in my fifteenth year. My father's family was proselyted to the Presbyterian faith…During this time of great excitement my mind was called up to serious reflection and great uneasiness…so great were the confusion and strife among the different denominations, that it was impossible for a person young as I was, and so unacquainted with men and things, to come to any certain conclusion who was right and who was wrong…I often said to myself, what is to be done? Who of all these parties are right; or, are they wrong altogether? (J. Smith, History of the Church 3-4)

Smith perhaps was referring to what became known as the "Burned Over District." It was a nickname given by historians to western and central New York in the early 1800's. At that time in that region there were steady streams of religious revivals. Smith certainly would not have been blind to them if they indeed occurred. In any case, young Joseph Smith was an opportunist.

He continued with his claim,

> While I was laboring under the extreme difficulties caused by the contests of these parties of religionists, I

was one day reading the Epistle of James, first chapter and fifth verse, which reads: If any of you lack wisdoim, let him ask of God, that giveth to all men liberally, and upbraideth not; and it shall be given him. Never did any passage of scripture come with more power to the heart of man than this did at this time to mine...I reflected on it again and again, knowing that if any person needed wisdom from God, I did...At length I came to the conclusion that I must remain in darkness and confusion or else I must do as James directs..." (J. Smith, History of the Church 4)

So it was in his same account Joseph described how he went into a grove of trees near his home and began to pray. However, no sooner had he begun than an evil and malignant force enveloped him and almost destroyed him.

He wrote,

> I was seized upon by some power which entirely overcame me, and had such an astonishing influence over me as to bind my tongue so that I could not speak. Thick darkness gathered around me, and it seemed to me for a time as if I were doomed to sudden destruction. But, exerting all my power to call upon God to deliver me out of the power of this enemy which had seized upon me, and at the very moment when I was ready to sink into despair and abandon myself to destruction – not to an imaginary ruin, but to the power of some actual being from the unseen world, who had such marvelous power as I had never before felt in any being – just at this moment of great alarm, I saw a pillar of light exactly over my head, above the brightness of the sun, which descended gradually until it fell upon me. It no sooner appeared than I found myself delivered from the enemy which held me bound. When the light rested upon me I saw two personages, whose brightness and glory defy all description, standing above me in the air. (J. Smith, History of the Church 5)

BREAKING THE CHAINS

The "darkness" was always described to me as being the power of Satan, who caused Joseph to be overwhelmed with fear and gloom. In contrast, the light of which he refers that ultimately saved him was God the Father and Jesus the Son who broke the darkness and came down in their "heavenly physical bodies." Smith wanted people to believe how God had given him special revelation pertaining to the Church and Smith would be the one to "restore" it. In 1823 he professes he was visited by an angel named Moroni who told him how many believed in God but did not have the truth. According to Smith, they lacked Priesthood authority to baptize and perform other laws. Then in 1827 the angel supposedly told him to go to a place called the Hill Cumorra. It was here where he would receive records written on gold plates in a language called Reformed Egyptian. Smith claims he translated them by the inspiration of God, and they would eventually become what is the Book of Mormon. On April 6, 1830 the Church of Jesus Christ of Latter Day Saints was organized and acknowledged in Fayette, New York under Joseph Smith.

DISCREPANCIES OF JOSEPH SMITH'S FIRST VISION ACCOUNT

There are several factors to consider when reading about the first vision. Smith's alleged encounter happened in 1820, yet was not officially documented until 1838, eighteen years after he claimed it happened. Joseph had conversations before 1838, but those accounts varied quite immensely.

Changing Accounts

The Doctrine and Covenants and Church History Seminar Teacher Manual reads,

> Joseph Smith wrote this account of the First Vision in 1838 as part of an official history of the Church to be published to the world. There are nine known accounts of the First Vision—four written or dictated by Joseph Smith and five written by others retelling his experience… The multiple accounts of the First Vision were prepared

at different times and for different audiences. In these accounts, Joseph Smith emphasized different aspects of his experience of the First Vision, but the accounts all agree in the essential truth that Joseph Smith did indeed have the heavens opened to him and see divine messengers, including God the Father and the Lord Jesus Christ. Because the 1838 account was part of Joseph Smith's official history and testimony to the world, it was included in the Pearl of Great Price as scripture. (p. 10)

The problem is the changes as confirmed by several recorded encounters and interviews neither agree in truth nor are consistent with his different audiences. He not only adds and deletes key details, but changes his story altogether until 1838.

The Institute for Religious Research has documented the numerous statements and changes made by Smith and his contemporaries pertaining to his testimony of the first vision story. In 1827 an account of Joseph Smith, Sr., and Joseph Smith, Jr. was given to Willard Chase, as related in his 1833 affidavit. Smith stated several years before obtaining the plates, a spirit appeared to him in a vision telling him of a record on gold plates. When he went to get the plates the spirit was in the form of a toad. It then transformed from toad to man and struck him twice and gave him instructions to come back again in a year. This was a command he said was repeated several years in a row. He said he was seventeen years old (1823) when the spirit first appears. At that point there was no mention of a revival. Smith also approached Martin Harris to say God has given Joseph a commandment and Harris should be the one to assist financially in producing the Book of Mormon.

In 1827 Martin Harris gave an account to the Reverend John A. Clark, as related in his 1842 book Gleanings by the Way. Again there was no mention of a revival. After an evening of money-digging, he said an angel appeared to Joseph in a vision telling him he has been chosen to be a prophet and bring forth a record on gold plates. Before Joseph can get them he must go to Pennsylvania to meet the woman who will be his wife. After marrying her Joseph must wait until the birth of his first child. Once the child had completed his second year Joseph could get the chest with the gold plates. Joseph was approximately age 18-19

BREAKING THE CHAINS

(1824-25) when the angel first appears (Joseph met Emma Hale in 1825 and married her Jan. 18, 1827). Joseph's first child was born and only six months old when he told his family about the vision. Instead of waiting the two years, Joseph disobeyed the angel and searched for the chest using his alleged clairvoyance. When he found it the angel appeared and Joseph was knocked to the ground and severely reprimanded.

The earliest known attempt at an "official" recounting of the 'First Vision was in 1832. It was reported Joseph determined all churches to be wrong. There was still no revival mentioned. This time he said he was fifteen years old. The location is not clear. He states he had a vision of the Savior Jesus Christ he described as a "Christian experience," who told him his sins were forgiven. At seventeen years old an angel who told him about the plates approached him.

In 1834-35 Oliver Cowdery, along with Joseph Smith's help, published the first history of Mormonism in the LDS periodical Messenger and Advocate. This time a revival is mentioned. He stated this vision happened in his bedroom.

There was an account in 1835-36 as found in his diary, Personal Writings of Joseph Smith. He tells of being in a grove at fourteen years old. But this time he had a vision of one personage and then another. One of the personages testified about Jesus, but neither is identified as Jesus. He claimed he saw many angels in this first visitation. Later, at seventeen years old, he says he had another vision of angels. There was no mention of a revival.

Joseph Smith gave an account to Erastus Holmes on November 14, 1835. It was originally published in the Deseret News on Saturday May 29, 1852, later published in the History of the Church, vol. 2, p. 312. It parallels the previously cited account and lends support to the view the dual personages in the 1835 diary account should be understood to be angels who affirm the Sonship of Jesus Christ rather than the Father and the Son. This supposedly happened when he was fourteen years old. He went to say how he had a vision of angels, and later revelations about the Book of Mormon.

Finally, the account of 1838 became the official version, now part of Mormon Scripture in the Pearl of Great Price, Joseph Smith —

History, 1:7-20. Though written in 1838, it was not published until 1842 in Times and Seasons, March 15, 1842, vol. 3, no. 10, pp. 727-728, 748-749, 753.

THERE WERE NO WITNESSES TO JOSEPH'S CLAIM

Another major discrepancy involves Joseph Smith as being the only witness to such an important event. The Gospel of Christ and the establishment of His church were never secretive. When Jesus was questioned of His disciples by a high priest He answers, "I spake openly to the world; I ever taught in the synagogue, and in the temple, whither the Jews always resort; and in secret have I said nothing." (Joh 18:20)

When Jesus appeared to His apostles following His death He explained to them,

> ...These are the words which I spake unto you, while I was yet with you, that all things must be fulfilled, which were written in the law of Moses, and in the prophets, and in the psalms, concerning me. Then opened he their understanding, that they might understand the scriptures, And said unto them, Thus it is written, and thus it behoved Christ to suffer, and to rise from the dead the third day: And that repentance and remission of sins should be preached in his name among all nations, beginning at Jerusalem. And ye are witnesses of these things [emphasis, NF]. (Luk 24:44-48)

When the Lord's church was established at Pentecost, there were many witnesses to it. Luke writes, "Parthians, and Medes, and Elamites, and the dwellers in Mesopotamia, and in Judaea, and Cappadocia, in Pontus, and Asia, Phrygia, and Pamphylia, in Egypt, and in the parts of Libya about Cyrene, and strangers of Rome, Jews and proselytes, Cretes and Arabians, we do hear them speak in our tongues the wonderful works of God. And they were all amazed, and were in doubt, saying one to another, What meaneth this?" (Act 2:9-12) There was never a time when anything so significant as revealing God's plan or establishing the kingdom was ever done privately.

BREAKING THE CHAINS
The Bible Was Alive and Well in the 1800's

As with all things, the Bible will defeat error and expose false teaching. How ironic Joseph's assertion to start questioning would be his greatest shortcoming. His mistake was quoting the Bible, which was obviously on the earth at the time the Church of Jesus Christ of Latter-day Saints was established. As such, God's word never left and His kingdom was never in jeopardy of being removed. Since Joseph Smith had the word of God in his possession, why would he need any further revealing of how to restore the church of the New Testament? He had access to the Bible. The many religions around him had access to it. Christ's true disciples had access to it up to that point. Why would God need to give a direct revelation to something already in the Bible? If that were the case, the revelation in the Bible is not sufficient. Joseph had a chance to adhere to it but chose not to do it.

Every time the Bible is preached, New Testament Christianity is restored. Restoration can happen individually or universally. John writes, "But if we walk in the light, as he is in the light, we have fellowship one with another, and the blood of Jesus Christ his Son cleanseth us from all sin." (1 Joh 1:7) The light of which this refers was not Mormon doctrine then, nor is it now. It is Christ's and is able to be found in the New Testament only. Paul writes of a Christian's focus and desire to stay faithful to the Law of Christ (1 Cor 9:24-27; Gal. 1:6; 5:4) The New Testament also refers to how a child of God can remove himself from Christ's church.

Peter writes,

> For if after they have escaped the pollutions of the world through the knowledge of the Lord and Saviour Jesus Christ, they are again entangled therein, and overcome, the latter end is worse with them than the beginning. For it had been better for them not to have known the way of righteousness, than, after they have known it, to turn from the holy commandment delivered unto them. But it is happened unto them according to the true proverb, The dog is turned to his own vomit again; and the sow that was washed to her wallowing in the mire. (2 Pet 2:20-22)

Peter's emphasis is to rebuke those who have changed the word of God and implore them to be restored to Christ's teachings.

There was likewise falling away by congregations and groups. Jesus warned the people in Asia, "Remember therefore from whence thou art fallen, and repent, and do the first works; or else I will come unto thee quickly, and will remove thy candlestick out of his place, except thou repent." (Rev 2:5) The same thing can happen to a plurality of congregations. Over time there were different groups who apostatized in different parts of the world in the form of denominations and cultic religions. Denominations sprang up individually from the efforts to reform Christ's church. Each one has taught different things, governs with different hierarchies, answer to different governing bodies, and hold different creeds. However, they only exist in relative harmony. Despite the intention of the reformers, their efforts failed Biblically.

When America was established there were already denominations filling the occupied land. Restoration was necessary, but there is a difference between restoration and reformation. The preachers of the American restoration movement had one purpose, to lead others out of denominations and back to following the New Testament only. They were instrumental in exposing the error of denominationalism.

In August 1801, 20,000 to 30,000 people flooded Cane Ridge, Kentucky for a major revival. Eighteen Presbyterian preachers along with Baptists, Methodists and other groups were among the crowd including Peter Cartwright, a famous Methodist preacher at the time. What was astonishing is people started responding to the preaching of the New Testament including Cartwright. Many realized the need universally to be born again and the means of salvation is the Gospel and not unconditional election. Barton W. Stone, who was on his way out of the Presbyterian Church preached the Gospel as a condition of salvation which got him in trouble with the Presbyterians. The Orothodox Presbytery considered Stone a heretic. Robert Marshall, Richard McNemar, John Dunlavy, and John Thompason were also under scrutiny with him. The five men left the Kentucky synod and set up a Presbytery of their own known as the Springfield Presbytery. They sent letters to churches describing their views and expressed total abandonment of all authoritative creeds except the Bible. Stone told congregations he no longer preached for the Presbyterian Church. He lost the friendship of two large congregations along with a large salary. Less than on year later, fifteen congregations were established at his hand. All five men realized the Presbytery had a party spirit and was a handicap to the work of restoring Bible authority. On June 28, 1804 they drafted The Last Will and Testament of the Springfield Presbytery. Robert Marshall, John Dunlavy, Richard McNemar, Barton W. Stone, John Thompson, and David Purviance signed it.

It reads,

> The Presbytery of Springfield sitting at Cane Ridge, in the county of Bourbon, being, through a gracious Providence, in more than ordinary bodily health, growing in strength and size daily; and in perfect soundness and composure of mind; but knowing that it is appointed for all delegated bodies once to die; and considering that the life of every such body is very uncertain, do make and ordain this our last Will and Testament, in manner and form following, viz.:
>
> ***Imprimis.*** We will, that this body die, be dissolved, and sink into union with the Body of Christ at large; for there is but one body, and one Spirit, even as we are called in one hope of our calling.
>
> ***Item.*** We will that our name of distinction, with its Reverend title, be forgotten, that there be but one Lord over God's heritage, and his name one.
>
> ***Item.*** We will, that our power of making laws for the government of the church, and executing them by delegated authority, forever cease; that the people may have free course to the Bible, and adopt the law of the Spirit of life in Christ Jesus.
>
> ***Item.*** We will, that candidates for the Gospel ministry henceforth study the Holy Scriptures with fervent prayer, and obtain license from God to preach the simple Gospel,

with the Holy Ghost sent down from heaven, without any mixture of philosophy, vain deceit, traditions of men, or the rudiments of the world. And let none henceforth take this honor to himself, but he that is called of God, as was Aaron.

Item. We will, that the church of Christ resume her native right of internal government,-- try her candidates for the ministry, as to their soundness in the faith, acquaintance with experimental religion, gravity and aptness to teach; and admit no other proof of their authority but Christ speaking in them. We will, that the church of Christ look up to the Lord of the harvest to send forth laborers into his harvest; and that she resume her primitive right of trying those who say they are apostles, and are not.

Item. We will, that each particular church, as a body, actuated b y the same spirit, choose her own preacher, and support him by a free-will offering, without a written call or subscription--admit members--remove offenses; and never henceforth delegate her right of government to any man or set of men whatever.

Item. We will, that the people henceforth take the Bible as the only sure guide to heaven; and as many as are offended with other books, which stand in competition with it, may cast them into the fire if they choose; for it is better to enter into life having one book, than having many to be cast into hell.

Item. We will, that preachers and people cultivate a spirit of mutual forbearance; pray more and dispute less; and while they behold the signs of the times, look up, and confidently expect that redemption draweth nigh.

Item. We will, that our weak brethren, who may have been wishing to make the Presbytery of Springfield their king, and wot not what is now become of it, betake themselves to the Rock of Ages, and follow Jesus for the future.

Item. We will, the Synod of Kentucky examine every member who may be suspected of having departed from the Confession of Faith, and suspend every such suspected heretic immediately, in order that the oppressed may go free, and taste the sweets of Gospel liberty.

Item. We will, that Ja--- -----, the author of two letters lately published in Lexington, be encouraged in his zeal to destroy partyism. We will, moreover, that our past conduct be examined into by all who may have correct information; but let foreigners beware of speaking evil of things which they know not.

Item. Finally we will, that all our sister bodies read their Bibles carefully, that they may see their fate there determined, and prepare for death before it is too late.

Springfield Presbytery, June 28th, 1804

Robert Marshall,}

John Dunlavy, }

Richard M'Nemar,}--Witnesses. B. W. Stone, }

John Thompson, }

David Purviance,}

Paul writes, "And the things that thou hast heard of me among many witnesses, the same commit thou to faithful men, who shall be able to teach others also." (2 Tim 2:2) The Gospel is a seed promulgated. It produces a Christian who produces a Christian who produces a Christian.

This is where Joseph Smith failed. Instead of restoring New Testament teaching based on what Christ and His apostles taught he came up with the Church of Jesus Christ of Latter-day Saints, having a doctrine and practice that could not be found anywhere in the Bible. By his own actions and admission he acknowledged the word of God and "all things that pertain unto life and godliness" (2 Pet 1:3) were never lost. Thus, he condemns himself. If he truly restored New Testament

Christianity like he claimed, there would be no room for Mormonism since there is no mention of it or its doctrine in the Bible. Instead he penned the Book of Mormon, Doctrine and Covenants, and Pearl of Great Price in which his so-called revelations would not only contradict previous "revelations," but habitually change. This is one of the dangers in accepting what people try to pass as new revelation. It not only gets tangled with what has been truthfully written, but it can change with the seasons to entertain new ideas not prescribed in the Bible.

Peter assures,

> Seeing ye have purified your souls in obeying the truth through the Spirit unto unfeigned love of the brethren, see that ye love one another with a pure heart fervently: Being born again, not of corruptible seed, but of incorruptible, by the word of God, which liveth and abideth for ever. For all flesh is as grass, and all the glory of man as the flower of grass. The grass withereth, and the flower thereof falleth away: But the word of the Lord endureth for ever. And this is the word which by the gospel is preached unto you (1 Pet. 1:22-25)

Peter did not say the word of the Lord will continue to be revealed, but what has been written will endure forever. God has said everything He needs to say about living godly lives and going to heaven. His word does not need changing; it does not need updating; certainly it does not need to be revealed in any new way, especially with Scripture contradicting the Bible.

At one point I asked how the word of God could just be wiped out from existence. The answers I received fell short of reason and complete explanation. Paul warns, the elders at Ephesus, "For I know this, that after my departing shall grievous wolves enter in among you, not sparing the flock." (Act 20:29) The apostle also advises Timothy, "Preach the word; be instant in season, out of season; reprove, rebuke, exhort with all longsuffering and doctrine. For the time will come when they will not endure sound doctrine; but after their own lusts shall they heap to themselves teachers, having itching ears; And they shall turn away their ears from the truth, and shall be turned unto fables." (2 Tim 4:2-4) Though Paul was mindful there would be some apostasy, he never stated there would be total apostasy. That is an assumption added by Joseph Smith. Additionally Christ boldly declares to Peter, "…on this rock I will build My church, and the gates of Hades shall not prevail against it." (Matt 16:18, NKJV) In other words, not even death (the Hadean realm) can overcome the church of Christ. Paul writes, "Now to Him who is able to do exceedingly abundantly above all that we ask or think, according to the power that works in us, to Him be glory in the church by Christ Jesus to all generations, forever and ever. Amen." (Eph 3:20-21) There would never be a time in which the Gospel or the church would be vacant from a generation.

James Talmadge, a modern day Mormon apostle, said, "If the alleged apostasy of the primitive Church was not a reality, The Church of Jesus Christ of Latter Day Saints is not the divine institution its name proclaims." (The Great Apostasy, preface, p. iii). If the "Great Apostasy" is true, the Gospel did not endure as promised. Isaiah confirms, "The grass withereth, the flower fadeth: but the word of our God shall stand for ever." (Isa 40:8) This is reiterated by Peter (1 Pet 1:24-25). In order for Mormonism to be true, it must be proven without error it is the church prophesied in the Old Testament (Isa. 2; Joel 2; Jer. 2) and fulfilled in the New Testament (Act 2). Otherwise it is a false religion like so many other impostors.

WORKS CITED

Ballard, Melvin Joseph. Three Degrees of Glory. Ogden: Zion's Printing and Publishing Co., 1922.

Seminaries and Institutes of Religion Curriculum Services. "The Great Apostasy." Doctrine and Covenants and Church HIstory Seminary Teacher Manual. Salt Lake City: The Church of Jesus Christ of Latter-day Saints, 2013. 8.

Smith, Joseph Fielding. Doctrines of Salvation. Vol. 1. n.d.

Smith, Joseph. History of the Church. Vol. 1. n.d.

History of the Church. Vol. 6. Salt Lake City: Deseret News Book Company, 1978. 7 vols.

History of the Church. Vol. I. Salt Lake City: The Deseret Book Company, 1978. VII vols.

Stack, Peggy Fletcher. "Mormon and Black: Grappling With a Racist Past." 7 June 2008. The Salt Lake Tribune. 20 May 2015 <http://www.sltrib.com>.

Unknown, Author. Apostasy. 2004. 23 August 2014 <www.lds.org>.

Race and the Priesthood. 20 May 2015 <http://www.lds.org/topics/race-and-the-priesthood>.

Young, Brigham. "Intelligence, Etc." Journal of Discourses 7 (1859): 290.

2

THE GODHEAD

The most instrumental belief in causing me to question the feasibility of the Church of Jesus Christ of Latter-day Saints and my own faith at the time was their teaching on the Godhead along with the scheme of redemption. I thought I had a firm understanding of God, but the more I studied and surveyed this area, the more I found myself having questions and noticing ample discrepancies with no sufficient answers given by teachers or those older than me. Eventually I realized if we could not comprehend who God is based on what has been revealed in the Bible, then any other area of study would be irrelevant.

GOD THE FATHER

The first Article of Faith proclaims, "We believe in God the eternal Father, and in his Son Jesus Christ, and in the Holy Ghost." Such a statement seems harmless on the surface, but is why it is necessary to define terms. The anomaly is they do not fully accept God is eternal.

Origin of God the Father

It was told to me and the other children early on God had a beginning just as we do. We were instructed there have been millions of gods, each having their origin of becoming exalted figures.

BREAKING THE CHAINS

Orson Pratt, an original member of the Quorum of Twelve Apostles in the LDS hierarchy, wrote,

> If we should take a million of worlds like this and number their particles, we should find that there are more Gods than there are particles of matter in those worlds. But the attributes of Deity are one; and they constitute the one God that the Prophets speak of, and that the children of men in all worlds worship. One world has a personal God or Father, and the inhabitants thereof worship the attributes of that God, another world has another, and they worship His attributes, and besides Him there is no other; and when they worship Him they are at the same time worshipping the same attributes that dwell in all the personal Gods who fill immensity. (Pratt, The Holy Spirit and the Godhead)

Joseph Smith, the first President and founder of the LDS faith wrote, "In the beginning, the head of the Gods called a council of the Gods; and they came together and concocted a plan to create the world and people it. When we begin to learn this way, we begin to learn the only true God,1 and what kind of a being we have got to worship." (J. Smith 349-50)

W.W. Phelps, a LDS songwriter, penned this hymn:

> "If you could hie to Kolob
>
> In the twinkling of an eye,
>
> And then continue onward
>
> With that same speed to fly,
>
> D'ye think that you could ever,
>
> Through all eternity,
>
> Find out the generation
>
> Where Gods began to be?"

THE GODHEAD

I was indoctrinated with the belief God lives near a distant planet called Kolob where he observes us on earth. It was fascinating to me. Thinking I could stare at the stars at night and wondering if God might be watching me back was mysterious yet astonishing to me. Trying to contemplate how many gods and worlds there must be out there kept me enamored as a young boy. Even more, I was taught the backstory of God the Father and how he was once human. That certainly grabbed my attention.

Allegedly there are millions of planets throughout the universe, each overseen by its own supreme being. On one of these planets a long time ago, a "spirit child" was conceived from parents of a divine nature. They named him Elohim. During the course of events, the human race was created and it was decided Elohim would be born to human parents to given him a physical body. Because he was obedient and completely yielded himself to their instruction, he was made a god and elevated to a deified state like his father before him.

He then served on a council of many other gods. Eventually Elohim took multiple wives and together they had "spirit children." God needed a place to put these children, which is why he created earth. A meeting was called by the council of the gods in order to figure out what do with all of the "spirit children." Two of the "spirit children present at this meeting were Elohim's two eldest sons, Jesus Christ and Lucifer. Elohim revealed his plan to create earth, where he would eventually send all of his spirit children to inhabit mortal bodies. Supposedly, Lucifer wanted full glory for himself in this plan and wanted to force everyone to obey and become gods. On the other hand, Jesus wanted to give them free agency and the ability to choose right from wrong. Lucifer angrily led some of the spirits to revolt against his father, Elohim. Elohim punished Lucifer by transforming him into the devil, and his followers became demons that would be unable to obtain fleshly bodies.

Milton R. Hunter, member of the First Council of the Seventy, explained,

> Mormon prophets have continuously taught the sublime truth that God the Eternal Father was once a mortal man who passed through a school of earth life similar to that through which we are now passing. He became

> God-an exalted being…Yet, if we accept the great law of eternal progression, we must accept the fact that there was a time when Deity was much less powerful than He is today… Thus He grew in experience and continued to grow until He attained the status of Godhood. (Hunter 104, 114-115)

Joseph Smith wrote,

> I will go back to the beginning before the world was, to show what kind of being God is. What sort of a being was God in the beginning? Open your ears and hear, all ye ends of the earth, for I am going to prove it to you by the Bible, and to tell you the designs of God in relation to the human race, and why He interferes with the affairs of man.
>
> God himself was once as we are now, and is an exalted man, and sits enthroned in yonder heavens! That is the great secret. If the veil were rent today, and the great God who holds this world in its orbit, and who upholds all worlds and all things by his power, was to make himself visible, I say, if you were to see him today, you would see him like a man in form—like yourselves in all the person, image, and very form as a man; for Adam was created in the very fashion, image and likeness of God, and received instruction from, and walked, talked and conversed with him, as one man talks and communes with another.
>
> In order to understand the subject of the dead, for consolation of those who mourn for the loss of their friends, it is necessary we should understand the character and being of God and how he came to be so; for I am going to tell you how God came to be God. We have imagined and supposed that God was God from all eternity. I will refute that idea, and take away the veil, so that you may see.
>
> These are incomprehensible ideas to some, but they are simple. It is the first principle of the Gospel to know for a certainty the Character of God, and to know that we may converse with him as one man converses with

another, and that he was once a man like us; yea, that God himself, the Father of us all,1 dwelt on an earth, the same as Jesus Christ himself did; and I will show it from the Bible. (J. Smith 345-46)

Brigham Young affirmed, "He is our Father-the Father of our spirits, and was once a man in mortal flesh as we are, and is now an exalted Being. How many Gods there are, I do not know. But there never was a time when there were not Gods and worlds, and when men were not passing through the same ordeals that we are now passing through." (Young)

B.H. Roberts, Member of the Quorum of the Seventy, wrote,

> But if God the Father was not always God, but came to his present exalted position by degrees of progress as indicated in the teachings of the prophet, how has there been a God from all eternity? The answer is that there has been and there now exists an endless line of Gods, stretching back into the eternities. (Roberts 476)

This incited me to ask the question if God was conceived, and his god before him was conceived, and his god before him was conceived, and so on, then who is the first God? No one could ever answer this question. I was told it was one of those mysteries of God. But I wanted answers.

Isaiah wrote, "…before Me there was no God formed, neither shall there be after Me. I, even I, am the LORD; and beside Me there is no saviour" (Isa. 43:10-11). Orson Pratt attempted to explain this by writing, "One world has a personal God or Father, and the inhabitants thereof worship the attributes of that God, another world has another, and they worship His attributes, and besides Him there is no other; and when they worship Him they are at the same time worshipping the same attributes that dwell in all the personal Gods who fill immensity" (Pratt, The Holy Spirit and the Godhead). Yet he fails to give attention to the rest of Isaiah's words: "…I am the first, and I am the last; and beside Me there is no God…Is there a God beside Me? yea, there is no God; I know not any" (Isa. 44:6, 8). If God were a man He would know other gods, yet in His omnipotence and omniscience He does not acknowledge any other period. Moses writes, "Lord, thou hast been our dwelling place in all generations. Before the mountains were brought forth, or ever thou hadst formed the earth and the world, even from everlasting to everlasting, thou art God." (Ps. 90:1-2) It is significant to observe if "to everlasting" is endless, then "from everlasting" must also be. The Bible will always be its own best interpreter, whether from immediate or remote context.

The first line of the Mormon sacramental prayer reads, "Oh God the eternal Father..." It was a prayer I uttered every week just before the sacrament was passed around to those in attendance. I never gave it much thought since it became so routine and I started questioning the nature of the Father. How could God be finite and infinite at the same time? I became frustrated with the lack of explanation from those around me. I was just searching for something to make sense and have it consistent with even itself. The more I questioned the more I realized how erratic their explanations were.

Nature of God the Father

This was one area definitely puzzling to me. I was always told in Sunday School classes God has a body of flesh and blood, but it's a "heavenly body." I would ask, "So we can't feel it?" They would say we could if we met Him. Then they read me something from the Doctrine and Covenants.

Smith wrote, "The Father has a body of flesh and bones as tangible as man's; the Son also; but the Holy Ghost has not a body of flesh and bones, but is a personage of Spirit. Were it not so, the Holy Ghost could not dwell in us" (Doctrines & Covenants 130:22). Likewise this is how they were described in Smith's alleged "first vision." Then it was physical, I had my answer...so I thought. One teacher of mine said it is physical but in a heavenly way. I asked what the difference was. He told me it's a "glorified body." I was back to the beginning of trying to decipher such cryptic answers. God is either physical or He is not. Just about every adult I would ask attempted to reconcile it by having me read Genesis. Moses writes, "So God created man in his own image, in the image of God created he him; male and female created he them." (Gen. 1:27) They would try to expound how the "image" was physical and God created man based on what He looked like. It did not take much for me to see how forced that answer seemed. Man was created with the ability to think, rationalize, plan, be creative, and reason. So is God.

Joseph F. Smith wrote, "The Father of our spirits is an eternal being with a body of flesh and bones. God has a tabernacle of flesh and bone. He is an organized being just as we are, who are now in the flesh...I do not believe in the doctrine held by some that God is only a Spirit..." (J. F. Smith) He should have believed Christ. Jesus states, "God is a Spirit: and they that worship him must worship him in spirit and in truth" (Jn. 4:24). When I asked about this, I was told this passage refers to the Holy Spirit. However, the preceding verse plainly clarifies this Spirit as the Father. Jesus corroborates this by explaining to His disciples upon His brief return a spirit does not have flesh and bones (Lk. 24:37-39). Paul writes, "Now this I say, brethren, that flesh and blood cannot inherit the kingdom of God; neither doth corruption inherit incorruption...For this corruptible must put on incorruption, and this mortal must put on immortality." (1 Cor. 15:50, 53) The word corruptible means "that which can decay." Thankfully, the Bible was there to clarify everything.

JESUS THE SON OF GOD

A critical error I believed about Jesus was how He was not always with God the Father. Rather, God the Father, Elohim, created Jesus who then became a part of the Godhead and was given a heavenly body. Milton Hunter proclaims in his book The Gospel Through the Ages, "Jesus became a God and reached His great state of understanding through consistent effort and continuous obedience to all the Gospel truths and universal laws." (Hunter, 51)

Robert L. Millett, former Dean of Religious Education at Brigham Young University, addressed the Harvard Divinity School in 2001, "We believe Jesus is the Son of God the Father and as such inherited powers of godhood and divinity from His Father, including immortality, the capacity to live forever. While He walked the dusty road of Palestine as a man, He possessed the powers of a God and ministered as one having authority, including power over the elements and even power over life and death." (Millett 14)

The belief Jesus was a created being is in serious violation of the word of God. Jesus emphatically states, "I am Alpha and Omega, the beginning and the ending, the first and last…" (Rev. 1:8, 11; 21:6; 22:13) John tells the Jews, "…Before Abraham was, I am." (Jn. 8:58) There is absolutely no evidence or sound Scripture corroborating the fallacy of Christ having a beginning.

CONCEPTION OF JESUS

Controversy within the LDS Church surrounds how Jesus became flesh and has caused quite a bit of division. As a child, I accepted Mary was a virgin, but through a miracle she was able to become pregnant with the Savior. However, a counter doctrine has grown suggesting God had sexual relations with His own creation in order for Jesus to have the capabilities He did. I have seen Mormons argue intensely on this subject, including members of my own family.

James E. Talmage, member of the Quorum of the Twelve Apostles, was quoted in Doctrines of the Gospel, "That child to be born of Mary was begotten of Elohim, the Eternal Father, not in violation of natural law but in accordance with a higher manifestation thereof; and, the offspring from that association of supreme sanctity, celestial sireship, and pure though mortal maternity, was of right to be called the 'son of the highest." (Talmage 9) The same manual quotes Heber J. Grant, the seventh President of the LDS Church, "We believe absolutely that Jesus Christ is the Son of God, begotten of God, the first-born in the spirit and the only begotten in the flesh; that He is the Son of God just as much as you and I are the sons of our fathers."

Ezra Taft Benson, the thirteenth President of the LDS Church, wrote,

> The Church of Jesus Christ of Latter-day Saints proclaims that Jesus Christ is the Son of God in the most literal sense. The body in which He performed His mission in the flesh was sired by that same Holy Being we worship

as God, our Eternal Father. Jesus was not the son of Joseph, nor was He begotten by the Holy Ghost. He is the Son of the Eternal Father…Jesus Christ is the Son of God. He came to this earth at a foreappointed time through a royal birthright that preserved His godhood. Combined in His nature were the human attributes of His mortal mother and the divine attributes of His Eternal Father. As the Son of God, He inherited powers and intelligence that no human has ever had before or since. (Benson 7-8)

Brigham Young wrote, "The birth of the Savior was as natural as are the births of our children; it was the result of natural action. He partook of flesh and blood—was begotten of his Father, as we were of our fathers." (Young 115)

Orson Pratt authored,

> The fleshly body of Jesus required a Mother as well as a Father. Therefore, the Father and Mother of Jesus, according to the flesh, must have been associated together in the capacity of Husband and Wife; hence the Virgin Mary must have been, for the time being, the lawful wife of God the Father: we use the term lawful Wife, because it would be blasphemous in the highest degree to say that He overshadowed her or begat the Saviour unlawfully. It would have been unlawful for any man to have interfered with Mary, who was already espoused to Joseph; for such a heinous crime would have subjected both the guilty parties to death, according to the law of Moses. But God having created all men and women, had the most perfect right to do with His own creation, according to His holy will and pleasure: He had a lawful right to overshadow the Virgin Mary in the capacity of a husband, and beget a Son, although she was espoused to another; for the law which He gave to govern men and women was not intended to govern Himself, or to prescribe rules for his own conduct. It was also lawful in Him, after having thus dealt with Mary, to giver her

> to Joseph her espoused husband. Whether God the Father gave Mary to Joseph for time only, or for time and eternity, we are not informed. Inasmuch as God was the first husband to her, it may be that He only gave her to be the wife of Joseph while in this mortal state, and that He intended after the resurrection to again take her as one of his own wives to raise up immortal spirits in eternity. (Pratt 158)

However, the Bible describes Christ very differently. The apostle John clarifies, "In the beginning was the Word, and the Word was with God, and the Word was God…And the Word was made flesh, and dwelt among us…" (Jn. 1:1, 14). The Word (Jesus) was God and was with God for all time and then made flesh. The term "made" is translated from the Greek word **ginomai** (ginomai) and refers to a change of state. It is "spoken of persons or things which receive any new character or form." (Zodhiates 369) He was not always of physical form but He has always been deity.

John explains, "And this is life eternal, that they might know thee the only true God, and Jesus Christ, whom thou hast sent. I have glorified thee on the earth: I have finished the work which thou gavest me to do. And now, O Father, glorify thou me with thine own self with the glory which I had with thee before the world was. (Jn. 17:3-5)

Not only is Jesus Spirit in nature, He is the Creator. John writes, "All things were made by him; and without him was not any thing made that was made. In him was life; and the life was the light of men." (Jn. 1:3-4) Paul also identifies Jesus as the Creator: "For by Him were all things created, that are in heaven, and that are in earth, visible and invisible…And He is before all things, and by Him all things consist" (Col. 1:16-17). It is impossible for a creator to create himself. Therefore Jesus, being the creator, has always been. He lives outside of time, which enables Him to create. For me it was vital to recognize if one cannot distinctly understand the nature of the Godhead, how can anything else be viable?

History of Christ on Earth

One of the things I believed for a long time during His earthly ministry is Jesus came to what was America at that point to teach the people. I remember learning how the Indians were really the Israelites and needed to hear the gospel. This provoked Jesus to visit Ancient America. The Book of Mormon states, "Ye are they of whom I said: Other sheep I have which are not of this fold." (3 Nephi 15:21) Everyone I knew understood this to mean the other fold meant American soil. It also states, "Behold, I am Jesus Christ, whom the prophets testified shall come into the world." (3 Nephi 11:10) This was especially exciting to hear. My goal was to locate where Jesus walked in America and trace His steps. I got caught up in the fantasy of living in a country where Jesus actually visited. But the evidence was clear.

John writes,

> I am the good shepherd, and know my sheep, and am known of mine. As the Father knoweth me, even so know I the Father: and I lay down my life for the sheep. And other sheep I have, which are not of this fold: them also I must bring, and they shall hear my voice; and there shall be one fold, and one shepherd." (Jn. 10:14-16)

It is important to understand the context. This was spoken to the Jews. Christ said there are other sheep "not of this [Jewish] fold." The other sheep not of the Jewish fold refers to the Gentiles. Christ was adamant His gospel would indeed be for all, not just the Jews. He came to establish one universal system for salvation. Paul writes, "There is neither Jew nor Greek, there is neither bond nor free, there is neither male nor female: for ye are all one in Christ Jesus. And if ye be Christ's, then are ye Abraham's seed, and heirs according to the promise." (Gal. 3:28-29) Isaiah prophesies, "I the Lord have called thee in righteousness, and will hold thine hand, and will keep thee, and give thee for a covenant of the people, for a light of the Gentiles." (Isa. 42:6) Micah records a prophecy regarding the church of Christ. He writes, "But in the last days it shall come to pass, that the mountain of the house of the Lord shall be established in the top of the mountains, and it shall be exalted above the hills; and people shall flow unto it, and many nations shall come, and say, Come, and let us go up to the mountain of the Lord, and to the house of the God of Jacob; and he will teach us of his ways, and we will walk in his paths: for the law shall go forth of Zion, and the word of the Lord from Jerusalem." (Mic. 4:1-2) In other words, Jew and Gentile would become one flock/church/kingdom.

Holy Spirit

Mormons are confused about the Holy Spirit like many denominations. Joseph Smith wrote, "The Father has a body of flesh and bones as tangible as man's; the Son also; but the Holy Ghost has not a body of flesh and bones, but is a personage of Spirit. Were it not so, the Holy Ghost could not dwell in us." (Doctrine & Covenants 130:22) In other words, I believed the Holy Spirit was able to literally dwell inside of an individual and guide him to the truth. I would tell people if they prayed longingly and had the faith, the Holy Spirit would direct them to know the Book of Mormon was true. Of course, my mind was already made up the Book of Mormon had to be the truth.

The Holy Spirit will not manifest anything because He has already done so, having given us the word of God. Contrary to what I believed, there does not need to be any more revelation for the truth. The Holy Spirit also cannot literally dwell in us as the passage suggests. John writes, "Howbeit when he, the Spirit of truth, is come, he will guide you into all truth: for he shall not speak of himself; but whatsoever he shall hear, that shall he speak: and he will shew you things to come." (Jn. 16:13) Notice a masculine pronoun given seven times in Christ's statement. He is not talking about a steam cloud or apparition or an element or ghostly figure. He is talking about a being just like Him. He is not an "It" but a being – a "He." He is the third person of the Godhead.

There are certain attributes to show He is a being. He can be blasphemed (Matt. 19:17). He teaches (1 Cor. 2:13; Jn. 14:26). This cannot be said of a vapor. He testifies (Jn. 15:26). He testified of the Christ to the inspired men. He is a guide (Jn. 16:13). He can be lied to (Acts 5:3). This shows he must be a personality albeit a spirit. He can be resisted (Acts 7:51). The Holy Spirit spoke through the prophets. He leads. He forbids (Acts 16:6-7). He has a mind (Rom. 8:27). He loves (Rom. 16:30).

Paul writes,

> But God hath revealed them unto us by his Spirit: for the Spirit searcheth all things, yea, the deep things of God. For what man knoweth the things of a man, save the spirit of man which is in him? even so the things of God knoweth no man, but the Spirit of God. Now we have received, not the spirit of the world, but the spirit which is of God; that we might know the things that are freely given to us of God. Which things also we speak, not in the words which man's wisdom teacheth, but which the Holy Ghost teacheth; comparing spiritual things with spiritual. (1 Cor. 2:10-13)

One can grieve Him (Eph. 5:30). He speaks (1 Tim. 4:1). He can be hated (Heb. 10:29). He intercedes (Rom. 8:27). All of these attributes lead to the conclusion that He is a being.

Additionally, the Holy Spirit already revealed what was meant for us. Jesus explains, "But the Comforter, which is the Holy Ghost, whom the Father will send in my name, he shall teach you all things, and bring all things to your remembrance, whatsoever I have said unto you." (Jn. 14:26) The Holy Spirit's job was to teach them all things. Peter writes, "According as his divine power hath given unto us all things that pertain unto life and godliness, through the knowledge of him that hath called us to glory and virtue:" (2 Pet. 1:3) They did not need any more. They had all things.

Paul writes, "All scripture is given by inspiration of God, and is profitable for doctrine, for reproof, for correction, for instruction in righteousness: 17 That the man of God may be perfect, throughly furnished unto all good works." (2 Tim. 3:16-17) All scripture is profitable and intended to teach, reprove, correct, instruct. If the word does this, what does the Holy Spirit do? Mormonism teaches the Holy Spirit does the correcting. They claim the Holy Spirit keeps us from sinning. But it is the word the Holy Spirit gave which is able to correct us. It is all-sufficient. Notice every time the Holy Spirit was present, a miracle occurred. How can He be present today and no miracles taking place?

BREAKING THE CHAINS

Every conversion in the book of Acts involved hearing and obedience of the word given by the Holy Spirit, but not an indwelling to "guide them into truth."

Notice the conversion of the Ethiopian eunuch:

> And the angel of the Lord spake unto Philip, saying, Arise, and go toward the south unto the way that goeth down from Jerusalem unto Gaza, which is desert. And he arose and went: and, behold, a man of Ethiopia, an eunuch of great authority under Candace queen of the Ethiopians, who had the charge of all her treasure, and had come to Jerusalem for to worship, Was returning, and sitting in his chariot read Esaias the prophet. Then the Spirit said unto Philip, Go near, and join thyself to this chariot. And Philip ran thither to him, and heard him read the prophet Esaias, and said, Understandest thou what thou readest? And he said, How can I, except some man should guide me? And he desired Philip that he would come up and sit with him. The place of the scripture which he read was this, He was led as a sheep to the slaughter; and like a lamb dumb before his shearer, so opened he not his mouth: In his humiliation his judgment was taken away: and who shall declare his generation? for his life is taken from the earth. And the eunuch answered Philip, and said, I pray thee, of whom speaketh the prophet this? of himself, or of some other man? Then Philip opened his mouth, and began at the same scripture, and preached unto him Jesus. And as they went on their way, they came unto a certain water: and the eunuch said, See, here is water; what doth hinder me to be baptized? And Philip said, If thou believest with all thine heart, thou mayest. And he answered and said, I believe that Jesus Christ is the Son of God. 38 And he commanded the chariot to stand still: and they went down both into the water, both Philip and the eunuch; and he baptized him. (Acts 8:26-38)

There was no special need of an indwelling of the Holy Spirit or any other supernatural means to understand the context. Neither was it needed for the conversion of the Philippian jailor (Acts 16:30-33). There was never a time when man needed the Holy Spirit to guide him to know what the Holy Spirit had already wanted him to know. Man has ten senses: five external and five internal. The five external are taste, smell, hearing, touch and sight. The five internal are perception (how we are acquainted with everything); reflection (I tasted something; I perceive what it is; now I can reflect on it); memory, reason, and judgment. Man knows there is a Holy Spirit because of the word. Man knows what that word is. He can rationalize that word. He knows nothing more than what has been revealed already. If the Holy Spirit leads man apart from what is already known in the Bible, He denies the Bible. He cannot directly make man a better Christian than what has already been given.

WORKS CITED

Benson, Ezra Taft. The Teachings of Ezra Taft Benson. Bookcraft, Inc., 1988.

Cannon, George Q. "LDS General Conference." Conference Report. unknown, 1900. 55-56.

Church of Jesus Christ of Latter-day Saints. "Gospel Fundamentals." 1992, 2002. The Church of Jesus Christ of Latter-day Saints. 24 August 2016 <http://www.lds.org>.

—. "Gospel Fundamentals." 1992, 2002. The Church of Jesus Christ of Latter-day Saints. 24 August 2016 <http://www.lds.org>.

Hunter, Milton R. The Gospel Through the Ages. Salt Lake City: Deseret Book Company, 1945.

Millett, Robert L. "What Mormons Believe About Jesus Christ." Mormon Newsroom. 14 September 2016 <http://www.mormonnewsroom.org/article/what-mormons-believe-about-jesus-christ>.

Pratt, Orson. "The Holy Spirit and the Godhead." Journal of Discourses 2 (1855): 334-347.

—. "The Holy Spirit and the Godhead." 18 February 1855. Journal of Discourses. 11 August 2016 <http://www.jod.mrm.org/2/334>.

—. The Seer. 1853.

Roberts, B.H. A New Witness for God. Vol. 1. Salt Lake City: George Q. Cannon & Sons Company, 1895.

Skinner, Andrew C. From Zion to Destruction: The Lessons of 4 Nephi. September 2000. 28 October 2014 <http://www.lds.org >.

Smith, Joseph Fielding. "Chapter 40: The Father and the Son." 2011. The Church of Jesus Christ of Latter-day Saints. 18 September 2016 <http://www.lds.org/manual/teachings-joseph-f-smith/chapter-40>.

Smith, Joseph Fielding Smith. Teachings of the Prophet Joseph Smith. 1838.

Smith, Joseph. Teachings of the Prophet Joseph Smith. Salt Lake City: Deseret Book Company, 1938.

Talmage, James. "Jesus Christ, the Son of God." Doctrines of the Gospel - Student Manual. Salt Lake City: CES Editing, 2010. 9.

Young, Brigham. "Character of God and Christ - Providences of God - Self Government, Etcc." Journal of Discourses. Vol. 8. Salt Lake City, 1860. 26 vols. 115.

—. "Progress in Knowledge, Etc." 8 October 1859. Journal of Discourses. 11 August 2016 <http://www.jod.mrm.org/7/331>.

—. "The Gospel of Salvation, Etc." Journal of Discourses 3 (1852): 93-94.

Zodhiates, Spiros. The Complete Word Study Dictionary, New Testament. Chattanooga: AMG Publishers, 1992.

3

HOW RELIABLE IS THE BOOK OF MORMON?

There are four books the Mormon Church believes are inspired canon. They are used regularly by them and are taught as historical and accurate scripture. Each one offers a different aspect of their theology. As I matured, I was instructed it was my responsibility to become acquainted with each one so I could share it with others.

The Book of Mormon is the most recognized of all books exclusive to LDS teaching. It supposedly covers the period from 600 B.C. to A.D. 421. On the cover it is identified as "Another Testament of Jesus Christ." Upon further examination of the most recent editions one will see it was "Translated by Joseph Smith, Jun." Another page just prior to its Introduction states how the first English edition was published in 1830. Rather than an extensive book of doctrinal matters, the Book of Mormon is more of their alleged historical account. It describes the life and descendants of a man named Lehi from Jerusalem and include some revelations. It covers the supposed past of ancient America.

The Doctrine and Covenants covers a period from 1823 to 1918. Its title page renders it as "Containing revelations given to Joseph Smith, the Prophet. With some additions by his successors in the presidency of the church." This is the book to read if one wants to know about much of the doctrinal issues. It includes details of the LDS Plan of Salvation. It lists numerous prophecies relevant to their leaders and key personnel.

BREAKING THE CHAINS

The Pearl of Great Price contains the Book of Moses and the Book of Abraham. Included are the famous Articles of Faith, which is a series of thirteen statements covering much of what the Mormon Church teaches. The Book of Abraham includes the Sensen Papyri, a collection of three pieces of papyrus allegedly detailing some of the life and demise of Abraham.

Finally, they hold to the King James Version of the Bible. Though it seems much the same as a standard KJV Bible, one will notice footnotes connecting it to their other works. They also do not give it as much attention as the Book of Mormon. The Eighth Article of Faith reads, "We believe the Bible to be the word of God as far as it is translated correctly…"

Together, these are the doctrinal books held as inspired and what define the LDS religion. They often can be found as either a triple volume set (Book of Mormon, Doctrine and Covenants, Pearl of Great Price), or even a quad which includes the Bible. Every child is given them early on and encouraged to get to know the content. Upon my baptism at eight years old, I was given the quadruple set and I thought it was a wonderful gift at the time. My name was engraved on the leather cover and I used it weekly, if not daily. This was church history as far as I understood.

My Mormon faith never caused me to abandon the Bible, but we always gave more credibility to the Book of Mormon. As a child, we were encouraged to read the Book of Mormon in its entirety, whereas the Bible was not nearly as emphasized. The eighth Article of Faith reads, "We believe the Bible to be the word of God as far as it is translated correctly; we also believe the Book of Mormon to be the word of God." There are a few things to consider with their statement. First, either the Bible (Genesis to Revelation) is the complete and only inspired word of God or it is not. If it is, then no religion has authority to teach or practice from any other source. If it is not the only inspired text, then the religious world must accept there may be other forms of inspired writings. If it is the case then the Book of Mormon may be what Joseph Smith declared it to be. However, when making a claim the Bible is the word of God "as far as it is translated correctly," they are implying the Bible, unlike the Book of Mormon, may have some unreliable text. It is important to realize then the burden of proof is placed on the shoulders of those making such an accusation. In other words, prove where the Bible is not translated correctly or is unreliable in terms of being the word of God. Their statement also places a significant rank on a book no other religion accepts as inspired canon.

Peter emphasizes, "For all flesh is as grass, and all the glory of man as the flower of grass. The grass withereth, and the flower thereof falleth away: But the word of the Lord endureth for ever. And this is the word which by the gospel is preached unto you" (1 Pet. 1:24-25). The gospel to which he refers is the same gospel preached throughout the Bible; not the Book of Mormon. In order to answer whether or not one can get to heaven obeying the Book of Mormon, one must examine if the Book of Mormon is inspired.

THE INSPIRATION OF THE BOOK OF MORMON IS UNRELIABLE

It Has a Human Author

The first edition of the Book of Mormon was officially released in the year 1830. Controversy surrounds the authorship, beginning with how it was published. On the title page of the original version, Joseph Smith is listed as "Author and Proprietor" when he registered the first edition in New York. If the Book of Mormon was indeed inspired by the Holy Spirit, why did Smith claim to be the author? Mormon apologists contend the copyright laws in New York, where the Book of Mormon was produced, stated one must list himself as such in order to prevent plagiarism. However, a careful study will reveal the law actually states, "Author" or "Proprietor" was sufficient. (Bracha)

Further, this law certainly did not apply to the printed testimony of eleven witnesses who attested Smith was both Author and Proprietor in the early edition of the book. Present day editions have deleted those testimonies. Eventually "Author and Proprietor" was replaced with "Translator" on the title page a few years later. So which is it? There is a vast difference between the role of an author and a translator. Why not just simply identify himself as "Translator," which was legal to do? If

Smith was the author then it ceases to be divine. If he was not, why did the eleven witnesses say differently? How can they be trusted? When a sworn testimony is changed, it becomes invalid or questionable at best. Three other assumed witnesses would be added: Oliver Cowdery, David Whitmer, and Martin Harris.

It Plagiarizes a Work of Fiction

More controversy would follow the authorship by way of a man named Solomon Spalding. Spalding was ordained a Congregationalist preacher in 1787 and later tried his hand at writing novels in the early 1800's. He was never successful, but in 1816 he wrote an unpublished historical romance about the lost civilization of the mound builders of North America titled Manuscript Found. It was authored fourteen years before the Book of Mormon was released. Its plot and character names are almost identical with the ones found in the Book of Mormon. Because of this many accused Smith of plagiarism, and using Spalding's work as the theme of the Book of Mormon.

Those in defense of the Book of Mormon have always stood firm it was nothing more than an attempt to discredit the Book of Mormon. For years the LDS Church was successful in dismantling most of the dispute. However, those who knew Spalding launched their own investigation claiming he was the source. Unfortunately, Spalding died before he had an opportunity to defend his work.

In 1976 three men, Wayne L. Cowdrey, Howard Davis, and Arthur Vanick, wrote a book titled Who Really Wrote the Book of Mormon? They exposed the original manuscript and had a handwriting analysis performed to see if the original copy of the Book of Mormon matched the original handwritten draft by Spalding. Many pages were confirmed as Spalding's, written verbatim into the Book of Mormon. Names, plots, and places were a match. There were also some significant persons who came forward to confirm the allegations.

John Spalding, brother of Solomon Spalding, attested,

> He then told me he had been writing a book, which he intended to have printed, the avails of which he

thought would enable him to pay all his debts. The book was entitled the "Manuscript Found," of which he read to me many passages. -- It was an historical romance of the first settlers of America, endeavoring to show that the American Indians are the descendants of the Jews, or the lost tribes. It gave a detailed account of their journey from Jerusalem, by land and sea, till they arrived in America, under the command of NEPHI and LEHI. They afterwards had quarrels and contentions, and separated into two distinct nations, one of which he denominated Nephites and the other Lamanites...I have recently read the Book of Mormon, and to my great surprize I find nearly the same historical matter, names, &c. as they were in my brother's writings. I well remember that he wrote in the old style, and commenced about every sentence with "and it came to pass," or "now it came to pass," the same as in the Book of Mormon, and according to the best of my recollection and belief, it is the same as my brother Solomon wrote, with the exception of the religious matter. -- By what means it has fallen into the hands of Joseph Smith, Jr. I am unable to determine. (Howe, Mormonism Unveiled 279-280)

Martha Spalding, the sister-in-law of Solomon, declared,

> I was personally acquainted with Solomon Spalding, about twenty years ago. I was at his house a short time before he left Conneaut; he was then writing a historical novel founded upon the first settlers of America. He represented them as an enlightened and warlike people. He had for many years contended that the aborigines of America were the descendants of some of the lost tribes of Israel, and this idea he carried out in the book in question. -- The lapse of time which has intervened, prevents my recollecting but few of the leading incidents of his writings; but the names of Nephi and Lehi are yet fresh in my memory, as being the principal heroes of his tale. They were officers of the company which first came off from Jerusalem. He gave a particular account of their

> journey by land and sea, till they arrived in America, after which, disputes arose between the chiefs, which caused them to separate into different lands, one of which was called Lamanites and the other Nephites. Between these were recounted tremendous battles, which frequently covered the ground with the slain; and their being buried in large heaps was the cause of the numerous mounds in the country. -- Some of these people he represented as being very large. I have read the Book of Mormon, which has brought fresh to my recollection the writings of Solomon Spalding; and I have no manner of doubt that the historical part of it, is the same that I read and heard read, more than 20 years ago. The old, obsolete style, and the phrases of "and it came to pass," &c. are the same. (Howe, Mormonism Unveiled 280-281)

John N. Miller, an employee of Solomon Spalding in 1811 asserted,

> I have recently examined the Book of Mormon, and find in it the writings of Solomon Spalding, from beginning to end, but mixed up with scripture and other religious matter, which I did not meet with in the "Manuscript Found." Many of the passages in the Mormon Book are verbatim from Spalding, and others in part. The names of Nephi, Lehi, Moroni, and in fact all the principal names, are bro't fresh to my recollection, by the Gold Bible. When Spalding divested his history of its fabulous names, by a verbal explanation, he landed his people near the Straits of Darien, which I am very confident he called Zarahemla, they were marched about that country for a length of time, in which wars and great blood shed ensued, he brought them across North America in a north east direction. (Howe, Mormonism Unveiled 283)

In 1833 Aaron Wright, a Justice of the Peace in Conneaut, affirmed,

> I first became acquainted with Solomon Spalding in 1808 or 9, when he commenced building a forge on Conneaut creek. When at his house, one day, he showed and read to me a history he was writing, of the lost tribes of Israel,

purporting that they were the first settlers of America, and that the Indians were their decendants. Upon this subject we had frequent conversations. He traced their journey from Jerusalem to America, as it is given in the Book of Mormon, excepting the religious matter. The historical part of the Book of Mormon, I know to be the same as I read and heard read from the writings of Spalding, more than twenty years ago; the names more especially are the same without any alteration. He told me his object was to account for all the fortifications, &c. to be found in this country, and said that in time it would be fully believed by all, except learned men and historians. I once anticipated reading his writings in print, but little expected to see them in a new Bible. Spalding had many other manuscripts, which I expect to see when Smith translates his other plate. In conclusion, I will observe, that the names of, and most of the historical part of the Book of Mormon, were as familiar to me before I read it, as most modern history. If it is not Spalding's writing, it is the same as he wrote; and if Smith was inspired, I think it was by the same spirit that Spalding was, which he confessed to be the love of money. (Howe, Mormonism Unveiled 284)

It Plagiarizes the King James Version of the Bible

Spalding's work was not the only text copied. There are also over forty plagiarisms Smith lifted directly from the King James Version of the Bible. These are not just similar passages of content. They are either verbatim or slightly varied in minor words. This was one of the ways our teachers attempted to harmonize the Book of Mormon with the Bible.

At the time I just accepted it as similar wording. However, the more I studied later the more it was evident the Book of Mormon contained nothing more than blatant duplicated passages taken out of their original context. The wording was sometimes modified by the arrogance or ignorance of Joseph Smith, often changing it to make no sense.

For example, Isaiah 2:9 reads, "And the mean man boweth down, and the great man humbleth himself: therefore forgive them not." Compare this to 2 Nephi 12:9 which reads, "And the mean man boweth not down, and the great man humbleth himself not, therefore, forgive him not." The preceding passage explains, "Their land also is full of idols; they worship the work of their own hands, that which their own fingers have made:" (Isa. 2:8) This is the reason the "mean man" and "great man" of Isaiah's rebuke were not to be forgiven. They were those who bowed down to idols instead of God. Smith's wording changes the entire context. In his words, those who refused to bow down to idols were not to be forgiven.

Another example contains a major geographical error by Smith. Isaiah 9:1 describes "the sea, beyond Jordan, in Galilee of the nations." It is a reference to the Sea of Galilee which the Jordan River feeds. In 2 Nephi 19:1 it reads, "the way of the Red Sea beyond Jordan in Galilee of the nations." The Red Sea is over 150 miles south of Galilee.

There are thirteen consecutive chapters of Isaiah inserted into the book of 2 Nephi. Two chapters of Isaiah are inserted into 1 Nephi. Two chapters of Isaiah are inserted into 3 Nephi. One chapter of Isaiah is inserted into the book of Mosiah for a total twenty chapters lifted from Isaiah alone.

Some of the plagiarisms involve the time frame of which certain events took place. Malachi records, "For, behold, the day cometh, that shall burn as an oven; and all the proud, yea, and all that do wickedly, shall be stubble: and the day that cometh shall burn them up, saith the LORD of hosts, that it shall leave them neither root nor branch." (Mal. 4:1) Compare this to 1 Nephi 22:15 which reads, "For behold, saith the prophet, the time cometh speedily that Satan shall have no more power over the hearts of the children of men; for the day soon cometh that all the proud and they who do wickedly shall be as stubble; and the day cometh that they must be burned." The writings of Malachi date back to approximately 430 B.C. which is 170 years after the dating of 1 Nephi 22 in which Smith alleges the people in the Book of Mormon crossed the ocean.

In another time discrepancy John the Baptist preaches, "And now also the axe is laid unto the root of the trees: therefore every tree which bringeth not forth good fruit is hewn down, and cast into the fire." (Matt. 3:10) Alma 5:52 identically reads, "Behold, the ax is laid at the root of the tree; therefore every tree that bringeth not forth good fruit shall be hewn down and cast into the fire." LDS doctrine dates the supposed writings of Alma to 83 B.C., a century before John the Baptist even began preaching. The letters of the apostle Paul would not have been available at the time the LDS Church claims Moroni was written, yet Moroni chapter ten borrows significantly from 1 Corinthians 12.

These are only a few of the many feeble and failed attempts to reconcile the errors of the Book of Mormon with the infallible Bible. Consider the translators of KJV were not inspired, nor did any of them claim to be such. Smith on the other hand was adamant he was inspired when he translated the Book of Mormon from "reformed Egyptian" contained in the "gold plates" to English.

King James Bible	*Book of Mormon*
Isaiah 2:1-22	2 Nephi 12:1-22
Isaiah 3	2 Nephi 13
Isaiah 4	2 Nephi 14
Isaiah 5	2 Nephi 15
Isaiah 6	2 Nephi 16
Isaiah 7	2 Nephi 17
Isaiah 8	2 Nephi 18
Isaiah 9	2 Nephi 19
Isaiah 10	2 Nephi 20
Isaiah 11	2 Nephi 21
Isaiah 12	2 Nephi 22
Isaiah 13	2 Nephi 23
Isaiah 14	2 Nephi 24
Isaiah 48	1 Nephi 20
Isaiah 49	1 Nephi 21
Isaiah 50	2 Nephi 7
Isaiah 51	2 Nephi 8
Isaiah 52	3 Nephi 20
Isaiah 53	Mosiah 14

BREAKING THE CHAINS

King James Bible	*Book of Mormon*
Isaiah 54	3 Nephi 22
Malachi 4:1	1 Nephi 22:15
Matthew 3:10	Alma 5:52
Matthew 5	3 Nephi 12
Matthew 6	3 Nephi 13
Matthew 7	3 Nephi 14
John 5:29	Helaman 12:26
1 Corinthians 12:4-11	Moroni 10:8-17
1 Corinthians 13:2-13	Moroni 7:44-48
1 Corinthians 15:58	Mosiah 5:15

The Book of Mormon allegedly covers a historical period from 600 B.C. to A.D. 421, yet it quotes directly from the KJV translated in A.D. 1611. This means only one of two conclusions can be made. Either the KJV translators copied from the Book of Mormon or the Book of Mormon copied from the KJV translators. Since the Book of Mormon would come into existence 200 years after the KJV was translated, the first theory can be eliminated. Mormon apologists claim God gave the same revelation in the Book of Mormon as He did in Palestine. Smith held his position of being an inspired translator, and God was using him to translate directly from "reformed Egyptian" to English. But why would God help him translate it into King James English? That was not the language in Palestine. It was also not the language in the 1830's in America.

Newsroom, a website for LDS resources, lists itself as the official resource for news media, opinion leaders, and the public. The website states, "It [Book of Mormon] has been described as the "keystone" of the Church of Jesus Christ of Latter Day Saints. From the beginning, Church members have accepted it as scripture. This does not mean the Book of Mormon replaces the Bible as scripture for members of the Church." (www.mormonnewsroom.org) Perhaps it does not replace it because it attempts to duplicate it. How peculiar it is the Bible does not contain one passage verifying any historical evidence in the Book of Mormon, yet the Book of Mormon is full of Bible content. The reason is if the Bible is true, then there is no room for Mormon doctrine or history.

The Information of the Book of Mormon is Unreliable

Joseph Smith supposedly translated the Book of Mormon from a heavy tome made of gold, commonly referred to in the LDS Church as the "gold plates." He claimed it was written in "Reformed Egyptian" hieroglyphics, a language no credible historian has ever validated. In order to translate he said he would need the help of the Urim and Thummim.

The official Mormon website indicates it was "an instrument prepared of God to assist man in obtaining revelation from the Lord and in translating languages." (www.lds.org) While the Urim and Thummim is found in the Old Testament, the Mormon description of them are completely different, as nowhere is mentioned the Urim and Thummim were used as translating devices. The New Illustrated Bible Dictionary defines them as "Gems or stones carried by the high priest and used by him to determine God's will in certain matters." Additionally, there is no record of them being used after the reign of David. Smith and his family were accused on many occasions of being involved in occultic practices.

David Whitmer, one of the Book of Mormon's supposed three main witnesses, would later describe how Smith actually claimed to have received his translating ability, by looking at stones from a well in which letters would appear in English. Whitmer wrote, "…Joseph Smith would put the seer stone into at hat, and put his face in the hat, drawing it closely around his face to exclude the light; and in the darkness the spiritual light would shine…" (Whitmer, An Address to All Believers in Christ 12) God's methods of revelation never endorsed an occultic practice of translation. Moreover, why or how would an archaic form of an Egyptian language end up on American soil? No Egyptian hieroglyphics have ever been connected to the American continent, the language was never used, and certainly not a fabricated version of it.

Located at the front of every Book of Mormon is a written testimony supposedly signed by Oliver Cowdery, David Whitmer, and Martin Harris. They supposedly saw the "gold plates" first hand and according to Mormon beliefs corroborated Smith's revelation. Mormon officials and members vow these testimonies have never changed. However, an investigation will show otherwise. Credible witnesses must have sound judgment, not be easily swayed, their character and reputation must be unquestionable, and all statements must agree over time. Otherwise they are untrustworthy. Consider all three witnesses were excommunicated from the Mormon Church at different times. Two of the three later returned, but their testimony could not be trusted. All three accounts varied over time. (Groat)

Eight other witnesses are also listed in the front of the Book of Mormon. What is important to realize is they were all either family members or close friends of the Smith and Whitmer family. All eight apostatized from the LDS Church. By 1847 none were a part of it. All eight had questionable accounts outside of what the Book of Mormon lists. They were known to be superstitious, believing in divining rods and magic. Later on they all said they saw the plates with "eyes of faith" but never actually saw the tangible plates. Smith even referred to them at one point as counterfeiters.

David Whitmer wrote,

> If you believe my testimony to the Book of Mormon; if you believe that God spake to us three witnesses by his own voice, then I tell you that in June, 1838, God spake to me again by his own voice from the heavens, and told me to separate myself from among the Latter-Day Saints, for as they sought to do unto me, so should it be done unto them." (Whitmer, An Address to All Believers in Christ)

Contemporaries of Martin Harris described him as having unstable religious convictions. (Groat)

Joseph Smith confidently contended, "I told the brethren that the Book of Mormon was the most correct of any book on earth, and the keystone of our religion, and a man would get nearer to God by abiding by its precepts, than by any other book." (Smith, History of the Church 461) If Smith really was inspired while translating and God was the author of the English production, there would certainly be no changes needed and no contradictions. But the Book of Mormon contains more than three thousand changes since the 1830 version. It also supplies a number of questions that cannot be reasonably explained.

For example, 1 Nephi 10:17 states, "...he spake by the power of the Holy Ghost; which power he received by faith on the Son of God." This was supposedly written between 600 – 592 B.C. Power was not given until the Day of Pentecost. Jesus tells His disciples, "...ye shall receive power, after the Holy Ghost is come upon you" (Act 1:8) The Messiah was expected but never referred to as the Son of God.

In 2 Nephi 1:3 the "land of promise" is mentioned. Mormon theologians explain it is a reference to America. This greatly differs from what the Bible teaches. The writer of Hebrews explains, "By faith Abraham, when he was called to go out into a place which he should after receive for an inheritance, obeyed; and he went out, not knowing whither he went. By faith he sojourned in the land of promise, as in a strange country, dwelling in tabernacles with Isaac and Jacob, the heirs with him of the same promise:" (Heb 11:8-9) America is never mentioned in the Bible, nor is there any geographical or archaeological evidence to suggest otherwise.

In 2 Nephi 25:19 it is written, "For according to the words of the prophets, the Messiah cometh in six hundred years from the time that my father left Jerusalem; and according to the words of the prophets, and also the word of the angel of God, his name shall be Jesus Christ, the Son of God." It is supposedly a prophecy of Jesus. A few key things need to be considered. First, Christ is not His last name. Christ is a position which translated means "the anointed one." Further, the first time Jesus' name is mentioned by an angel is when Gabriel appears to Mary (Luk 1:31). Isaiah prophecies, "...and his name shall be called Wonderful, Counsellor, The mighty God, The everlasting Father, The Prince of Peace." (Isa. 9:6) Again, there is a substantial flaw in the dating.

Mosiah 2:3 describes how the people would "Offer sacrifice and burnt offerings according to Law of Moses," referring to the "Nephites" and "Lamanites." The challenge here is those two groups are, according to Mormonism's history, from the tribe of Manasseh. Only the tribe of Levi could give attendance at the altar (Exo 28 – 31). Moses writes, "And the LORD spake unto Moses, saying, Bring the tribe of Levi near, and present them before Aaron the priest, that they may minister unto him. And they shall keep his charge, and the charge of the whole congregation before the tabernacle of the congregation, to do the service of the tabernacle" (Num 3:5-7).

Mosiah 18:17 suggests, "And they were called the church of God, or the church of Christ, from that time forward…" This would normally sound acceptable, except it was supposedly written 145 B.C. It would be impossible for anyone to belong to Christ's church since it was not yet established. Christ set up His kingdom after His resurrection and on the Day of Pentecost (Act 2). Jesus said years after the Book of Mosiah was supposedly dated, "…upon this rock I will [emphasis added, NF] build my church…" (Matt 16:18)

Alma 46:15 asserts all those who were believers in Christ were called Christians. However, the Book of Alma was supposedly written 73 B.C. Luke's letter to Theophilus confirms the first time anyone was called a Christian was at Antioch (Act 11:26). The term "Christian" was never mentioned or recognized in the Old Testament. As a side note, the name Alma who the Mormons suggest was a mighty prophet of old, is translated in Hebrew as "betrothed maiden virgin."

The Evidence of the Book of Mormon is Unreliable

The final chapter of the Book of Mormon contains a "test" to confirm inspiration. It reads, "And when ye shall receive these things I would exhort you that ye would ask God, the Eternal Father, in the name of Christ, if these things are not true; and if ye shall ask with a sincere heart, with real intent, having faith in Christ, he will manifest the truth of it unto you, by the power of the Holy Ghost. And by the power of the Holy Ghost ye may know the truth of all things." (Moroni 10:4-5)

Members of the Mormon Church urge prospective converts to pray and ask God if it is true and the Holy Spirit will guide them to believing the Book of Mormon. The problem is it is a loaded approach. Many have read and followed their formula, only to conclude the Book of Mormon is false. Those in defense of the Mormon faith will simply say one does not have enough faith and to pray more. But their judgment is only viable if it is assumed already the Book of Mormon is the authority.

M. Russell Ballard, a current member of the Quorum of the Seventy, said in an interview when asked about the legitimacy of the Book of Mormon, "God has never revealed religious truth to the heart and soul of a man or woman except by the power of the Spirit…You will not get to know it by trying to prove it archeologically or by DNA or by anything else in my judgment. Just pick it up and read it and pray about it and you will come to know religious truth is always confirmed by what you feel and that's the way Heavenly Father answers prayers." (Ballard) I believed it for a long time until I realized what I feel might not be truth. It does not matter how much I pray or convince myself something is true, there has to be some sort of standard of authority. Otherwise I am the standard which is dangerously close to humanism. Solomon writes, "Trust in the LORD with all thine heart; and lean not unto thine own understanding." (Prov. 3:5) I knew if I wanted answers, they would have to come from more than just a feeling.

Christianity is based on evidence. There has never been a time in Biblical history when evidence could not be found. John writes, "That which was from the beginning, which we have heard, which we have seen with our eyes, which we have looked upon, and our hands have handled, of the Word of life." (1 Jn. 1:1) The apostles were able to verify Christ using sight, hearing and touch. It was how they were able to testify to others reasonably.

The same letter reads, "Beloved, believe not every spirit, but try the spirits whether they are of God: because many false prophets are gone out into the world (1 Jn. 4:1) It would be impossible to try the spirits without reliable evidence because there would be nothing of which to compare the doctrine. Luke records, "These were more noble than those in Thessalonica, in that they received the word with all readiness of mind, and searched the scriptures daily, whether those things were so." (Acts 17:11) Paul commended the Bereans based on their scrutinizing the Scriptures. They did not just have a feeling. Paul writes, "Prove all things; hold fast that which is good." (1 Thes. 5:21)

Paul emphasizes in his treatise to the Romans, "For the invisible things of him from the creation of the world are clearly seen, being understood by the things that are made, even his eternal power and Godhead; so that they are without excuse: Because that, when they knew God, they glorified him not as God, neither were thankful; but became vain in their imaginations, and their foolish heart was darkened." (Rom. 1:20-21) The pagans were without excuse because they refused to accept the evidence available to them by means of sense perception. They were vain in their reasoning.

Consider how many times Christ asked, "Have ye not read?" (Matt. 12:3, 5; 19:4; 22:31; Mk. 12:10, 26) He was telling them to recall the evidence was accessible to them. Paul writes, "For whatsoever things were written aforetime were written for our learning, that we through patience and comfort of the scriptures might have hope." (Rom. 15:4)

All of these references and more reveal the inspired writers relied on evidence to authenticate Scripture. Evidence of Christ as the One who fulfilled prophecy pricked the hearts of 3000 Jews on Pentecost and caused them to give up 1500 years of religious tradition. They saw, they heard, and they responded by repenting and being baptized for the remission of their sins. "…And the Lord added to the church daily such as should be saved." (Acts 2:47) It was not the Mormon Church that day, nor any denomination

If the Book of Mormon was destroyed, mankind could restart it. Why? It was man made. The same can not be said of the Bible. There are many tangible traces found to verify Biblical accounts. The Bible can be proved with archaeology, geographical settings, writings of ancient people and civilizations, cities, tools, weapons, and remains. It is what makes the Bible a priceless history book as well as the source connecting us with the One who created everything. It took me a long while to finally accept it.

If the Book of Mormon is not the divine revelation Smith and his church claim it to be, then the entire foundation of Mormonism crumbles under its own error and will get no one to heaven. The Bible on the other hand, is God breathed. Paul writes, "All scripture is given by inspiration of God, and is profitable for doctrine, for reproof, for correction, for instruction in righteousness." (2 Tim. 3:16)

Paul also writes, "There is one body, and one Spirit, even as ye are called in one hope of your calling; One Lord, one faith, one baptism." (Eph. 4:4-5) Books of Mormon theology can only be true if their doctrine is unmistakably in unison with what Bible teaches. Otherwise there is not "one body" or "one faith." The one faith provides hope of eternal salvation. The one faith enables people to be correctly added to the one body. The one faith keeps people in the grace of God as long as they remain obedient. The one faith has been tested and proven to be true time after time.

WORKS CITED

Ballard, M. Russell. "Transcript of Interview with M. Russell Ballard." 2 October 2007. The Church of Jesus Christ of Latter-day Saints. 28 September 2016 <http://www.mormonnewsroom.org>.

Bracha, O. Commentary on Copyright Act (1790). 2008. 29 May 2014 <www.copyrighthistory.org>.

Budge, Wallis. The Mummy, a Handbook of Egyptian Funerary Archaeology. New York: Dover Publications, 1989.

Groat, Joel. Facts On the Book of Mormon Witnesses - Part 1. 1996. 29 May 2014 <www.irr.org>.

Hines, Mark. Book of Abraham Fraud. 29 April 2015 <http://www.conchisle.com>.

Howe, E.D. Mormonism Unveiled. Painesville: Author, 1834.

—. Mormonism Unveiled. Painesville: Author, 1834.

—. Mormonism Unveiled. Painesville: Author, 1834.

—. Mormonism Unveiled. Painesville: Author, 1834.

Mathie, Kevin. Examining the Book of Abraham, Chapter 6. 6 May 2015 <http://www.bookofabraham.com>.

Rhodes, Michael D. I Have a Question. July 1988. 29 April 2015 <http://www.lds.org>.

Rhodes, Michael. Why Doesn't the Translation of Egyptian Papyri Found in 1967 Match the Text of the Book of Abraham in Pearl of Great Price? 1988. 6 May 2015 <http://www.lds.org/

ensign/1988/07/i-have-a-question>.

Ritner, Robert. Breathing Permit of Horus. 29 April 2015 <http://www.user.xmission.com/~research/breathing/index.htm>.

Smith, Joseph. History of the Church. Vol. II. Salt Lake City: The Deseret Book Company, 1978. VII vols.

—. History of the Church. Vol. 4. Salt Lake City: Deseret News, 1978. 7 vols.

Tanner, Sandra. Fall of the Book of Abraham. 29 April 2015 <http://www.utlm.org>.

Whitmer, David. An Address to All Believers in Christ. Richmond, 1837.

—. An Address to All Believers in Christ. Richmond, 1837.

4

OFFICES AND PRIESTHOODS

    The LDS Church ordains and installs men into certain offices set up as a hierarchy of sorts. They also acknowledge and ordain Priesthoods for men they deem qualified. However, Scripture must be inspected and evidence weighed to see if these positions are authorized today as they were in the past. If so, it is critical to examine the qualifications to be sure they are in accordance with what has been sanctioned by God. A careful investigation of their church organization will determine such.

DEACONS

    When I turned twelve years old, I was ordained as a Deacon, which is the standard age. Along with others my age, we were given the responsibility to distribute the Sacrament (communion) and collect "fast offerings" every Sunday morning. We would typically use sandwich bread or something similar, not thinking whether it had to be unleavened or not. We used water instead of fruit of the vine to represent Christ's blood. The adults would explain the reason we did it was because wine had alcohol and we were not permitted to have strong drink.

    It is also at this age I was ordained with the Aaronic Priesthood. It was a great honor in my mind to be acknowledged as a Deacon and those young men with whom I served understandably felt a sense of purpose. But once more, what does the Bible say about who is qualified?

Paul writes, "And let these also first be proved; then let them use the office of a deacon, being found blameless. Even so must their wives be grave, not slanderers, sober, faithful in all things. Let the deacons be the husbands of one wife, ruling their children and their own houses well." (1 Tim. 3:10-12) How many children at the age of twelve are married, have children, and their own houses? This inconsistent and erroneous disregard for Bible authority cannot be ignored if one wishes to follow New Testament teaching.

PRIESTS IN THE AARONIC PRIESTHOOD

When I turned sixteen years old I was ordained to the office of a Priest in the Aaronic Priesthood. Whereas a deacon would simply distribute the sacrament, a Priest had the privilege to administer, or bless, the sacrament each Sunday. Before serving each one there was a set prayer we would recite found in the Doctrine and Covenants.

The prayer for the bread reads,

> O God, the Eternal Father, we ask thee in the name of thy Son, Jesus Christ, to bless and sanctify this bread to the souls of all those who partake of it, that they may eat in remembrance of the body of thy Son, and witness unto thee, O God, the Eternal Father, that they are willing to take upon them the name of thy Son, and always remember him and keep his commandments which he has given them; that they may always have his Spirit to be with them. Amen. (Doctrine & Covenants 20:77)

The prayer for the cup (water) reads,

> O God, the Eternal Father, we ask thee in the name of thy Son, Jesus Christ, to bless and sanctify this wine to the souls of all those who drink of it, that they may do it in remembrance of the blood of thy Son, which was shed for them; that they may witness unto thee, O God,

the Eternal Father, that they do always remember him, that they may have his Spirit to be with them. Amen. (Doctrine & Covenants 20:79)

We also had the opportunity to give talks (preach) in the worship assembly, or Sacrament meeting. It was a great honor for us, as it made us feel like we were moving up in the ranks. All of us were granted the chance to speak and were greatly encouraged by the members to keep doing it. Perhaps the most memorable authority I had as a Priest was to baptize. We were granted this entitlement after being ordained by the Bishop. This was a great honor and I felt important after baptizing one of my younger brothers. Unbeknownst to me was the fact there is no Biblical authority to appoint a certain person special permission to baptize.

ELDERS

Elders are ordained by Mormon authorities and refer to any holder of the Melchizedek Priesthood, especially male missionaries. Young men are confirmed at eighteen or nineteen years old. The Doctrine and Covenants describe the duties of an Elder which include administering their Sacrament, baptizing, leading meetings, and confirming those who are baptized into the Mormon Church (D&C 20:38-45). They are correct Elders serve today, but are in error when it comes to the qualifications.

When Paul left Titus in Crete he instructs, "...set in order the things that are wanting, and ordain elders in every city, as I had appointed thee: If any be blameless, the husband of one wife, having faithful children not accused of riot or unruly. For a bishop must be blameless, as the steward of God..." (Tit. 1:5-7). There are a few significant variables. Are the young missionaries married? Do they have not just children but faithful children? If not, why are they labeled as "Elders?" Most when asked this question either do not know or they say it is just a title. But why do something different than what the Bible explicitly commands? Paul gives the same instruction to Timothy. He writes, "A bishop then must be...the husband of one wife...One that ruleth well his own house, having his children in subjection with all gravity"

(1 Tim. 3:2, 4). Again, where is the authority for a young single missionary to be given the title of an Elder?

Some in the Mormon Church attempt to argue an Elder and Bishop are two separate positions. However, a careful study of the context and usage of the original language will settle the discussion. There are three terms in the New Testament describing the same office: Elder, Bishop, and Pastor. Elder comes from the Greek word "presbuteros" and describes those Christians who presided over the assemblies (Strong). It is the same word used for "Presbyter" and is used in Titus 1:5 and 1 Peter 5:1. Bishop comes from the Greek word "episkopos" and is described as an "overseer." It is used in 1 Timothy 3:1 and Acts 20:28. Pastor comes from the Greek word "poimen." It is described as a "shepherd, overseer of the assembly, or a protector." It is used in Ephesians 5:11. Enhanced Strong's Dictionary, Easton's Bible Dictionary, and Vine's Expository Dictioanry of New Testament Words all confirm the three offices are used interchangeably in the New Testament. The International Standard Bible Encyclopedia states, "That "elders" and "bishops" were in apostolic and sub-apostolic times the same, is now almost universally admitted; in all New Testament references their functions are identical."

PROPHET

One man holds the office of President of the Church, also referred to as the Prophet. The Church of Jesus Christ of Latter Day Saints place unconditional trust and employs valued reverence to its leaders. Through the years Mormons have appointed different Prophets. Each generation has one who speaks for the Mormon Church. He is also the president of the Melchizedek Priesthood and sustained as prophet, seer, and revelator. Mormons believe he receives revelation for their church, in addition to the whole world. When he dies, another is chosen to take his place. He is recognized as the Prophet over the whole earth. He is the only one "authorized" to speak for God to all God's people. He is viewed the same as the prophets who can be found in the Bible. Those who assist him are called the First Presidency and the Quorum of the Twelve, also known as modern day "apostles". When there is not a Prophet on the earth, the Mormon Church calls it an apostasy.

OFFICES AND PRIESTHOODS

It is a time of darkness, and God must call a prophet to restore His church. Joseph Smith was called just like Moses was called, according to Mormonism.

Joseph Smith was their first Prophet and esteemed highly in their organization. John Taylor, a member of the Council of the Twelve, wrote:

> Joseph Smith, the Prophet and Seer of the Lord, has done more, save Jesus only, for the salvation of men in this world, than any other man that ever lived in it. In the short space of twenty years, he has brought forth the Book of Mormon, which he translated by the gift and power of God, and has been the means of publishing it on two continents; has sent the fullness of the everlasting gospel, which it contained, to the four quarters of the earth; has brought forth the revelations and commandments which compose this book of Doctrine and Covenants, and many other wise documents and instruction for the benefit of the children of men; gathered many thousands of the Latter-day Saints, founded a great city, and left a fame and name that cannot be slain. He lived great, and he died great in the eyes of God and his people; and like most of the Lord's anointed in ancient times, has sealed his mission and his works with his own blood; and so has his brother Hyrum. In life they were not divided, and in death they were not separated (Doctrine and Covenants 135:3)!

The following citations can be seen displayed at Temple Square on various plaques throughout its visitor center:

> We revere Joseph Smith as a prophet who testified of Jesus Christ and taught us to worship Christ as our Savior…Just as prophets before him, Joseph Smith and his successors received revelation from the Lord that became scripture. Some of these revelations are found in two books of modern-day scripture called the Doctrine and Covenants and the Pearl of Great Price. These books of scripture show us that God continues to

> give revelation to guide His children…Just as in Bible times, The Church of Jesus Christ of Latter-day Saints is led today by living prophets and apostles. They receive revelation from God, perform His work, and teach the gospel of Jesus Christ…God continues to call prophets. God continues to guide followers of Jesus Christ in our day through modern-day prophets. The Lord chose Joseph Smith to be a prophet and revealed to him the plan for His children. Like Moses, Isaiah, and other biblical prophets, Joseph Smith also saw God and was called by Him to preach His word.

The merit of praise has been debated among many historians. Smith in various articles has been recorded as being a money digger (treasure hunter) and a troublemaker, he had pending lawsuits and warrants for his arrest because of swindling, and he was arrested and tried for his disorderly conduct by the state of New York. Peter Ingersoll, a close acquaintance of Joseph Smith, appeared before Judge Thomas P. Baldwin of Wayne Country Court in Palmyra, Wayne County, New York on December 9, 1833. He testified in a sworn affidavit and affirmed under oath:

> One day he [Joseph Smith] came and greeted me with a joyful countenance. Upon asking the cause of his unusual happiness, he replied in the following language, 'As I was passing, yesterday, across the woods, after a heavy shower of rain, I found, in a hollow, some beautiful white sand, that had been washed up by the water. I took off my frock, and tied up several quarts of it, and then went home.
>
> On my entering the house, I found the family at the table eating dinner. They were all anxious to know the contents of my frock. At that moment, I happened to think of what I had heard about a history found in Canada, called the golden Bible; so I very gravely told them it was the golden Bible. To my surprise, they were credulous enough to believe what I said. Accordingly I told them that I had received a commandment to let no one see it, for, says I, no man can see it with the naked eye and live.

However, I offered to take out the book and show it to them, but they refuse to see it, and left the room.' Now, said Joe, 'I have got the damned fools fixed, and will carry out the fun.' Notwithstanding, he told me he had no such book and believed there never was any such book, yet, he told me that he actually went to Willard Chase, to get him to make a chest, in which he might deposit his golden Bible. But, as Chase would not do it, he made a box himself, of clapboards, and put it into a pillow case, and allowed people only to lift it, and feel of it through the case. (Ingersoll)

Eventually Joseph and his brother Hyrum ended up in jail in Carthage, Illinois. On June 27, 1844 an angry mob stormed where they were held and murdered both of them. It is difficult to convince those grounded in their Mormon beliefs of accepting Smith's controversial past. Most of them consider it as merely propaganda. Instead they choose to believe another history.

In order to determine whether there are prophets living today it is imperative to evaluate the purpose of a prophet and if any more revelations from God are needed today. Moses writes, "I will raise them up a Prophet from among their brethren, like unto thee, and will put my words in his mouth; and he shall speak unto them all that I shall command him" (Deut. 18:18-19). Obviously back then people needed prophets to reveal God's message, as God spoke through them. Hosea writes, "I have also spoken by the prophets, and have multiplied visions; I have given symbols through the witnesses of the prophets" (Hos. 12:10, NKJV). God used Prophets to guide His people in the right direction. A Prophet was a forthteller and foreteller. They prophesied during the time of the old covenant, as well as in the first century under the new covenant.

Prophecy was a miracle, and its purpose was to confirm the word (Heb. 2:1-4). Under New Testament, the apostles had the ability given by God to lay hands on people in order to impart a miraculous gift. Miracles such as prophecy are like scaffolding to a building. Once the building is complete, there is no more need for scaffolding. Such was the case with prophets (Cates 27-29). Paul talked about wanting the best gifts (1 Cor. 12:31). However, there was coming a time when all of it would end. Paul wrote, "Charity never faileth: but whether there be prophecies, they shall fail; whether there be tongues, they shall cease; whether there be knowledge, it shall vanish away" (1 Cor. 13:8). Notice prophecy would fail. Tongues would cease. A supernatural type of knowledge would vanish away. The only thing still in effect would be love. Paul continued, "For we know in part, and we prophesy in part. But when that which is perfect is come, then that which is in part shall be done away" (1 Cor. 13:9-10). That which is "in part" refers to the sharing of imperfect knowledge and includes prophecy, tongues, and miraculous knowledge. That which is "in part" will be done away. It would be the end of the miraculous gifts. Why? It is because they would no longer be needed. It does not mean they only had part of the truth. If that were the case, then when the "perfect" came then part of the truth would be done away. What was "done away" was the "in part" system of delivering truth. The "perfect" (complete) word of God would be revealed and completely delivered. The "perfect" in this text is not the Christ, as Christ had already come and ascended back to heaven. Paul said there would not always be a need for prophets. He then offered an analogy: "When I was a child, I spake as a child, I understood as a child: but when I became a man, I put away childish things" (1 Cor. 13:11). He put away childish things as the church would put away the needs of a prophet and miraculous gifts. "For now we see through a glass darkly; but then face to face: now I know in part; but then shall I know even as also I am known" (1 Cor. 13:12).

APOSTLES

Mormonism also ordains modern day Apostles. The Quorum of the Twelve Apostles (aka "First Presidency") are given all the keys. However, the President of the Church is the senior Apostle and is the only one able to use all of the keys given, according to them. The other Apostles act under his directorship. But does the Bible give room to appoint men of these positions today?

The apostles of Christ were walking New Testaments. When power from the Holy Spirit came upon the apostles on the day of Pentecost, they were brought to know "all things" (Joh. 14:26; cf 2 Pet. 1:3). They had the knowledge, even though they did not fully understand it all yet [for instance, Peter said the promise was for "all that are afar off" (i.e. Gentiles, cf. Act. 2:39), but it was a matter of years before the early Christians comprehended this fact (Act. 10)]. God gave the knowledge to mankind, but there was only so much the apostles could share at any one time. Consider a teacher cannot teach everything he knows on a subject in a given day, week, or semester. Likewise it took time for all of the information God shared with the apostles to be shared and applied, which was done against the backdrop of first century events the church faced. That which was "in part" was not the information being shared, but the method of delivery and distribution. That which was "perfect" was the method of delivery that would endure through the ages: the written Word of God

By the time Jude wrote Christians must "earnestly contend for the faith which was once delivered unto the saints" (Jude 3), the faith had been delivered. It was complete. There was no room for any other doctrine, including Mormonism, to be integrated with it. The time of the last person living able to prophesy was at the end. There were no apostles after to impart any more. The world had what it needed to live faithfully. Anything beyond that would be too much, or nothing more than recycled principles. John's Revelation would be a writing of hope and victory if the faith system was obediently and strictly followed.

Joseph Fielding Smith (Joseph Smith, Jr.'s nephew) wrote, "Mormonism, as it is called, must stand or fall on the story of Joseph Smith. He was either a prophet of God, divinely called, properly appointed and commissioned, or he was one of the biggest frauds this world has ever seen. There is no middle ground" (Smith). How close he was to the truth, as Biblical research along with secular evidence and testimonies would corroborate the latter part of his statement.

AARONIC PRIESTHOOD

There are two priesthoods in the Mormon Church, the Melchizedek and Aaronic which includes the Levitical (Doctrine & Covenants 107:1). The lesser of the two in terms of authority is the Aaronic, which functions under the direction of the Melchizedek. A male member at the age of twelve may receive the Aaronic Priesthood, which consists of the offices of Bishop, Priest, Teacher, and Deacon.

The Mormon Church teaches the Aaronic Priesthood was removed from the earth as part of their "Great Apostasy" doctrine, but was restored at a later date. A plaque titled Restoration of the Aaronic Priesthood located on the grounds of Temple Square in Salt Lake City, Utah reads:

> On May 15, 1829, Joseph Smith and Oliver Cowdery went into the woods to inquire of the Lord concerning baptism. As they prayed, "a messenger from heaven descended in a cloud of light" (Joseph Smith – History 1:68). This messenger was John the Baptist, who had baptized Jesus Christ in the River Jordan and was now a resurrected being. He laid his hands on Joseph and Oliver and conferred upon each them the Aaronic Priesthood. This priesthood, which had been absent from the earth for many centuries, includes the restored authority from God to baptize for the remission of sins.

There are several factors to consider upon such a claim. First, all Priests were Levites but not all Levites were Priests. John the Baptist never held the Aaronic (Levitical) Priesthood. Further, the priesthood of Aaron was never connected to baptism for the remission of sins. It had to do with the Mosaic Law. It was not lost to the "Great Apostasy." It was absent because Christ removed it and there was a reason. Paul writes concerning the Law of Moses, "Blotting out the handwriting of ordinances that was against us, which was contrary to us, and took it out of the way, nailing it to his cross" (Col. 2:14).

The Hebrew writer contends,

> If therefore perfection were by the Levitical priesthood, (for under it the people received the law,) what further need was there that another priest should rise after the order of Melchisedec, and not be called after the order of Aaron? For the priesthood being changed, there is made of necessity a change also of the law. For he of whom these things are spoken pertaineth to another tribe, of which no

man gave attendance at the altar. For it is evident that our Lord sprang out of Juda; of which tribe Moses spake nothing concerning priesthood (Heb. 7:11-14).

If only those who are Priests of the tribe of Aaron have the authority to baptize, then why could John the Baptist who was not a Priest? Why could Paul? The apostle never held that office, nor was he even a descendant of that tribe. Paul identifies himself as being of the tribe of Benjamin (Phi. 3:5), yet he was able to baptize (1 Cor. 1:14-16; Act 19:1-5). In fact there is no genealogical proof any of the other apostles held that priesthood or were of the tribe of Levi, but Christ commanded them to go and "teach all nations, baptizing them in the name of the Father, and of the Son, and of the Holy Ghost" (Mat. 28:19). Again, this is because baptism for the remission of sins was never connected to the Levitical duties.

Mormonism's alleged history also draws a discrepancy regarding tasks. The responsibilities of the Levitical priesthood included the teaching of the Law (Lev. 10:11); offering sacrifices (Lev. 9ff); tending to the Tabernacle and Temple (Num. 18:1-3); officiating in the Holy Place (Exo. 30:7-10); inspecting those who were ceremonial unclean (Lev. 13 – 14); adjudicated disagreements and arguments (Deu. 17:8-13). The Book of Mormon attaches Nephi and his offspring to the tribe of Joseph: "And thus my father, Lehi, also found upon the plates of brass a genealogy of his fathers; wherefore he knew that he was a descendant of Joseph; yea, even that Joseph who was the son of Jacob, who was sold into Egypt, and who was preserved by the hand of the Lord, that he might preserve his father, Jacob, and all his household from perishing with famine" (1 Nephi 5:14). Just prior to this they claim this same tribe "did offer sacrifice and burnt offerings unto the Lord; and they gave thanks unto the God of Israel" (1 Nephi 5:9). This was obviously a contradiction of the tribe who was authorized for such. There are several references to the severe consequences of those who defied God's strict laws pertaining to the Israelites' functions. Why wasn't Nephi or Lehi or any of their children punished? Not only that, but where in the Biblical list of genealogies for the different tribes is listed Nephi or Lehi? God was very specific in who would do what. Did He purposefully or conveniently leave them out?

Additionally, the priesthood of Aaron could only be held based on genealogy, or those who were of the lineage of Levi. Ezra discusses an account where some were stripped of the priesthood because they could not prove their lineage. He writes, "And of the children of the priests: the children of Habaiah, the children of Koz, the children of Barzillai; which took a wife of the daughters of Barzillai the Gileadite, and was called after their name: These sought their register among those that were reckoned by genealogy, but they were not found: therefore were they, as polluted, put from the priesthood" (Ezra 2:62). For argument sake, if it is the case the Levitical Priesthood could be held after the death of Christ (which the Bible plainly shows otherwise), then when the Mormons claim Joseph Smith and Oliver Cowdery had the Aaronic Priesthood given to them, every person holding the Aaronic Priesthood in the Mormon Church nowadays would have to be of the descent of Smith and/or Cowdery. It is of course absurd to accept all members of the Mormon faith are somehow related to one of the two families. This is further evidence of the inconsistent and chaotic reasoning to try to reestablish a priesthood deliberately taken out of the way by Christ.

Melchizedek Priesthood

Those in the LDS Church may also hold the Melchizedek Priesthood. The Doctrine and Covenants reveals,

Why the first is called the Melchizedek Priesthood is because Melchizedek was such a great high priest. Before his day it was called the Holy Priesthood, after the Order of the Son of God. But out of respect or reverence to the name of the Supreme Being, to avoid the too frequent repetition of his name, they, the church, in ancient days, called that priesthood after Melchizedek, or the Melchizedek Priesthood. All other authorities or offices in the church are appendages to this priesthood. But there are two divisions or grand heads—one is the Melchizedek Priesthood, and the other is the Aaronic or Levitical Priesthood. The office of an elder [not a missionary, NF] comes under the priesthood of Melchizedek. The Melchizedek Priesthood holds the right of presidency, and has power and authority over all the offices in the church in all ages of the world, to administer in spiritual things. The Presidency of the High Priesthood, after the order of Melchizedek, have a right to officiate in all the offices in the

OFFICES AND PRIESTHOODS

church. High priests after the order of the Melchizedek Priesthood have a right to officiate in their own standing, under the direction of the presidency, in administering spiritual things, and also in the office of an elder, priest (of the Levitical order), teacher, deacon, and member (Doctrine & Covenants 107:2-10).

Mormonism teaches the Melchizedek Priesthood, also called the "Holy Priesthood," was first held by Adam and continues through all generations (Doctrine & Covenants 89:6-17). However, they also claim it was removed from the earth for a period of time. Joseph Smith proclaimed he and Oliver Cowdery received the "restoration of the Melchizedek Priesthood."

A plaque at Temple Square reads:

> The Melchizedek Priesthood is the authority of God to lead His Church, give the gift of the Holy Ghost, and perform other saving ordinances. This authority has been on the earth whenever the Lord has revealed His gospel. It was lost from the earth after the death of Jesus's Apostles, but it was restored in May 1829, when the Apostles Peter, James, and John conferred it upon Joseph Smith and Oliver Cowdery. In the ordinances of the Melchizedek Priesthood, "the power of godliness is manifest" (Doctrine and Covenants 84:20).

These assertions made by Smith illustrate either a confusion or was ignorant in his knowledge of the Melchizedek Priesthood. David writes concerning Christ, "The Lord hath sworn, and will not repent, Thou art a priest for ever after the order of Melchizedek" (Psa. 110:4).

The Hebrew writer clarifies,

> Which hope we have as an anchor of the soul, both sure and stedfast, and which entereth into that within the veil; Whither the forerunner is for us entered, even Jesus, made an high priest for ever after the order of Melchisedec [emph., NF]. For this Melchisedec, king of Salem, priest of the most high God, who met Abraham returning from the slaughter of the kings,

> and blessed him; To whom also Abraham gave a tenth part of all; first being by interpretation King of righteousness, and after that also King of Salem, which is, King of peace; Without father, without mother, without descent, having neither beginning of days, nor end of life; but made like unto the Son of God; abideth a priest continually. Now consider how great this man was, unto whom even the patriarch Abraham gave the tenth of the spoils (Heb. 6:20 – 7:4).

Notice Christ is Priest after the order of Melchizedek. "After the order" in the original language means concerning the same style or nature as Melchizedek. In other words, like Melchizedek He is a Priest appointed without lineage. Christ is simply being compared to him. However, it was never intended to be for all time as the Doctrine & Covenants purports.

Again the Hebrew writer makes clear,

> If therefore perfection were by the Levitical priesthood, (for under it the people received the law,) what further need was there that another priest should rise after the order of Melchisedec, and not be called after the order of Aaron? For the priesthood being changed, there is made of necessity a change also of the law. For he of whom these things are spoken pertaineth to another tribe, of which no man gave attendance at the altar. For it is evident that our Lord sprang out of Juda; of which tribe Moses spake nothing concerning priesthood (Heb. 7:11-14).

The Melchizedek Priesthood ceases to exist today because it was taken out of the way at the cross. Why would God withhold something so vital for so long if it was lost? Notice the authority was for Christ. There is no authority today for the Melchizedek Priesthood to exist. The Hebrews writer emphasized how God was proving Jesus and Christianity was superior to Melchizedek. Peter writes, "But ye are a chosen generation, a royal priesthood, an holy nation, a peculiar people; that ye should shew forth the praises of him who hath called you out of darkness into his marvellous light: Which in time past were not a people, but are now the people of God: which had not obtained mercy, but now have obtained mercy" (1 Pet. 2:9-10).

Christians are under the priesthood of Christ. If Mormons want to bring back Priesthood which operated under the Law of Moses, they must bring back all of the Law to be consistent. Further, where in the Bible was there ever the authority to live under multiple priesthoods? The Israelites certainly had no authority and there was never any indication of them ever wanting it.

The Mormon system of offices and priesthoods is a tangled mess of inconsistent principles and guidelines. Their books contain many commandments on which a Mormon's hope to reach the Celestial Kingdom (the highest level of their depiction of Heaven) is contingent, but a close examination makes it a futile hope. God on the other hand has always been organized and precise in His plan. There is no room or leeway given to muddle its simple structure.

LAYING ON OF HANDS AND RECEIVING BLESSINGS

According to the Mormon Church, the laying on of hands is a procedure given by God to ordain special authorities and assign tasks for certain callings. Those holding the proper "priesthood" authority place their hands on the person's head receiving the words or special recognition. Those administering the act are seen as instruments through whom the Lord uses. I was both a recipient and an administrator of this ritual. It is common for a newborn baby to be brought forward and to have a few men stand with the father who holds the baby while giving him or her a "blessing." The blessing usually consists of a prayer that God will watch over and protect the baby in life, and they will grow to be strong in the Mormon Church.

Another time in which men will take part in laying on of hands is a baptism confirmation. A person is confirmed a member of the Church of Jesus Christ of Latter-day Saints after their baptism by a Mormon priesthood holder who puts his hands on the head of the person and blesses him or her to "receive the Holy Ghost."

BREAKING THE CHAINS

Laying On Of Hands For The Gift Of The Holy Ghost

It is difficult to get a satisfactory answer from anyone in the Mormon faith when asking about the gift of the Holy Ghost, much less the laying on of hands to receive it.

Joseph B. Wirthlen, a member of the LDS Quorum of the Twelve Apostles, writes,

> The Prophet Joseph Smith explained: "There is a difference between the Holy Ghost and the gift of the Holy Ghost. Cornelius received the Holy Ghost before he was baptized, which was the convincing power of God unto him of the truth of the Gospel, but he could not receive the gift of the Holy Ghost until after he was baptized. Had he not taken this ... ordinance upon him, the Holy Ghost which convinced him of the truth of God, would have left him." The gift of the Holy Ghost, which is the right to receive the Holy Ghost as a constant companion, is obtained only upon condition of faith in Christ, repentance, baptism by immersion, and the laying on of hands by authorized servants endowed with the Melchizedek Priesthood. It is a most precious gift available only to worthy members of the Lord's Church. In the Doctrine and Covenants, the Lord calls the gift of the Holy Ghost "the unspeakable gift." (D&C 121:26) It is the source of testimony and spiritual gifts. It enlightens minds, fills our souls with joy (D&C 11:13), teaches us all things, and brings forgotten knowledge to our remembrance. The Holy Ghost also "will show unto [us] all things what [we] should do." (Wirthlin)

None of this cooperates with Bible explanation. The Holy Spirit has revealed what everyone needs to do through the word of which He inspired the writers. Those who received the Holy Spirit received it by the miraculous abilities. It enabled them to perform miracles. A good example of this is when Peter and John entered Samaria (Act 8). Only the apostles had the authority to lay hands on others to receive these miraculous gifts. The same Greek form also applies to Acts 2:38 and Acts 10:45. Those who received the gift from the apostles were able to perform miracles. If anyone were to receive it the same way today they would be able to do the same miracles as described in the New Testament.

The purpose of miracles were to confirm the word (Heb. 2:1-4). Under New Testament, the apostles had the ability given by God to lay hands on people in order to impart a miraculous gift. Miracles such as prophecy are like scaffolding to a building. Once the building is complete, there is no more need for scaffolding. Such was the case with prophets (Cates 27-29). Paul talked about wanting the best gifts (1 Cor. 12:31). However, there was coming a time when all of it would end. Paul wrote, "Charity never faileth: but whether there be prophecies, they shall fail; whether there be tongues, they shall cease; whether there be knowledge, it shall vanish away" (1 Cor. 13:8). Notice prophecy would fail. Tongues would cease. A supernatural type of knowledge would vanish away. The only thing still in effect would be love. Paul continued, "For we know in part, and we prophesy in part. But when that which is perfect is come, then that which is in part shall be done away" (1 Cor. 13:9-10). That which is "in part" refers to the sharing of imperfect knowledge and includes prophecy, tongues, and miraculous knowledge. That which is "in part" will be done away. It would be the end of the miraculous gifts. Why? It is because they would no longer be needed. What was "done away" was the "in part" system of delivering truth. The "perfect" (complete) word of God would be revealed and completely delivered. The "perfect" in this text is not the Christ, as Christ had already come and ascended back to heaven. Paul said there would not always be a need for prophets. He then offered an analogy: "When I was a child, I spake as a child, I understood as a child: but when I became a man, I put away childish things" (1 Cor. 13:11). He put away childish things as the church would put away the needs of a prophet and miraculous gifts. "For now we see through a glass darkly; but then face to face: now I know in part; but then shall I know even as also I am known" (1 Cor. 13:12).

Laying On Of Hands To Preach

The fifth item of the LDS Articles of Faith states, "We believe that a man must be called of God, by prophecy, and by the laying on of hands by those who are in authority, to preach the Gospel and administer in the ordinances thereof." In other words, in order to preach the Gospel of Christ and be active in that roll, men serving in authoritative positions in the Church of Jesus Christ of Latter Day Saints must ordain or confirm him. When I was a teenager, it included being interviewed by the Bishop of the ward (congregation) to see if I was ready and worthy to meet such an important "calling." He would ask personal and general questions before declaring me worthy.

Loren C. Dunn, who held a seat on the First Council of the Seventy, stated in a speech:

> …This is part of the revealed procedure in the gospel of Jesus Christ, which takes place from the general to the ward or branch level and which allows every member the opportunity of sustaining a person who has been called to office…The Lord, then, gives us the opportunity to sustain the action of a divine calling and in effect express ourselves if for any reason we may feel otherwise. To sustain is to make the action binding on ourselves and to commit ourselves to support those people whom we have sustained. When a person goes through the sacred act of raising his arm to the square, he should remember, with soberness, that which he has done and commence to act in harmony with his sustaining vote both in public and in private… A calling in the Church is both a personal and a sacred matter, and everyone is entitled to know he or she has been called to act in the name of God in that particular position. Every person in this church has the right to know that he has been called of God. If he does not have that assurance, then I would suggest he give his calling serious, prayerful consideration so that he can receive what he has a right to receive. (Dunn)

Mr. Dunn's speech is an adequate representation of the LDS beliefs on this subject. Notice the hierarchy, which determines the validity of the "calling." But where is the authority for it to be done this way? If God calls man to preach the Gospel as Dunn admits, then why is it not sufficient? Why are there more needed, and why is it necessary for man to "sustain" anything, especially in such a ritualistic format?

Christ simply and directly told His eleven disciples, "…All power is given unto me in heaven and in earth. Go ye therefore, and teach all nations, baptizing them in the name of the Father, and of the Son, and of the Holy Ghost: Teaching them to observe all things whatsoever I have commanded you: and, lo, I am with you alway, even unto the end of the world" (Matt. 28:18-20). The disciples were given the calling: go and teach. What was to be their material? Jesus said to teach everything He had commanded them. There was never a "confirmation" or "sustaining" ritual preceding their preaching the Gospel or fulfilling the ordinances (laws). No one was called upon to lay hands on them. The only authority involved was Christ, and doing things in the name of the Godhead.

Consider the time after Christ defeated death and appeared to His eleven as they ate. He commands them, "Go ye into all the world, and preach the gospel to every creature…" (Mar 16:16). Again, there is no mention or hint of the need for anyone in authority laying hands on them to preach. They were sustained by the word itself and the commandment. Additionally, the only confirmation mentioned were the miracles performed to confirm what they spoke was truth.

The apostle Paul, who labored continuously for the kingdom of God, imparted sound teaching to Timothy: "And the things that thou hast heard of me among many witnesses, the same commit thou to faithful men, who shall be able to teach others also. Thou therefore endure hardness, as a good soldier of Jesus Christ" (2 Tim. 2:2-3). He did not lay hands on him, though he did teach him. There was no ceremony or ritual. Timothy was told to take what he had learned from Paul, which was the Gospel of Christ, and teach it to faithful men so they could teach others. The word "faithful" is derived from the Greek word pistoj (pistos) which means "trusting" or "agreeable". It is certainly the case when the Great Commission is fulfilled today. The Gospel cannot and will not reach those who are unwilling to hear it.

In another part of the same letter Paul tells Timothy, "Preach the word; be instant in season, out of season; reprove, rebuke, exhort with all longsuffering and doctrine" (2 Tim. 4:2). There was no ritual, no formality, no special ceremony. Paul told him to preach and Timothy was expected to do it. The only authority came from the One whose doctrine he was to preach.

BREAKING THE CHAINS

There are so many instances throughout the inspired writings of the New Testament alluding to preaching and teaching, yet none require someone in an authoritative position to lay hands and "confirm" them before they are able to do it. They were simply taught and became disciples upon their confession of Christ, repenting, and being baptized into His name so to be added to His church. The only times the laying on of hands is mentioned in the New Testament in an evangelistic context is when the apostles would bestow miraculous gifts to one or more. Its purpose was to confirm the glory of God and God's power. Since those days of miracles have ceased (1 Cor. 13), one must be careful not to add something to God's word that is not there.

PATRIARCHAL BLESSINGS

If I had been a member of the LDS Church just a little while longer I would have received my Patriarchal Blessing, which is a declaration of a person's lineage as it pertains to the house of Israel and includes personal counsel from God. Every person who is judged worthy and has been baptized is entitled to receive it.

Thomas Monson (current President of the LDS Church) writes,

> As a person studies his or her patriarchal blessing and follows the counsel it contains, it will provide guidance, comfort, and protection. A patriarchal blessing includes a declaration of lineage, stating that the person is of the house of Israel—a descendant of Abraham, belonging to a specific tribe of Jacob. Many Latter-day Saints are of the tribe of Ephraim, the tribe given the primary responsibility to lead the latter-day work of the Lord." Because each of us has many bloodlines running in us, two members of the same family may be declared as being of different tribes in Israel.
>
> It does not matter if a person's lineage in the house of Israel is through bloodlines or by adoption. Church members are counted as a descendant of Abraham and an heir to all the promises and blessings contained in the

Abrahamic covenant... Those who follow the counsel in their patriarchal blessing will be less likely to go astray or be misled. Only by following the counsel in a patriarchal blessing can one receive the blessings contained therein. the recipient of the blessing should not assume that everything mentioned in it will be fulfilled in this life. A patriarchal blessing is eternal, and its promises may extend into the eternities. If one is worthy, all promises will be fulfilled in the Lord's due time. Those promises and blessings that are not realized in this life will be fulfilled in the next. Patriarchal blessings are sacred and personal. They may be shared with immediate family members, but should not be read aloud in public or read or interpreted by others. Not even the patriarch or bishop or branch president should interpret it. Those who have received a patriarchal blessing should treasure its words, ponder them, and live to be worthy to receive the promised blessings in this life and in the life to come. (Monson)

There are a few shortcomings in receiving such identification. First, mankind is no longer under the Patriarchal dispensation. As of the cross, the only priesthood or authority one is subject to today is Christ. Second, since the records for the Jewish lineage were kept in the temple in Jerusalem and the temple was destroyed in A.D. 70 during the destruction, the records would have been lost.

WORKS CITED

Cates, Curtis. "Does the Holy Spirit Work Miraculously?" Pillars - The Holy Spirit. Duluth: Rampart Productions, 2007. 27-29.

Dunn, Loren C. We Are Called of God. April 1972. 15 April 2014 <http://www.lds.org/general-conference/1972/04/we-are-called-of-god?>.

Ingersoll, Peter. "Peter Ingersoll Statement on Joseph Smith, Jr." Truth and Grace. 27 June 2013 <http://www.truthandgrace.com/statementIngersoll1.htm>.

Monson, Thomas. Patriarchal Blessings. 13 May 2015 <http://www.lds.org>.

Smith, Joseph Fielding. Doctrines of Salvation. Vol. 1. n.d.

unknown, Author. Priesthood. 3 December 2012. 30 April 2014 <http://www.mormonwiki.com/Priesthood>.

Wirthlin, Joseph B. The Unspeakable Gift. May 2003. 5 Mar 2014 <http://www.lds.org>.

5

ESCHATOLOGY

Eschatology is a fascinating study but one often mishandled. Most are curious by how the world will end and how quickly certain occurrences will unfold. It is important those seeking truth do not presume anything or add something not contained in the Bible. This is typically what leads many to get confused. Religious leaders get caught up in the "fantasy" of the end of the world. In turn they seek to educate inquiring members or students with their beliefs rather than simply present what the Bible says. The Church of Jesus Christ of Latter-day Saints have developed several tenets that have guided and continue to guide its members into a corrupted web of error.

One of the things that genuinely scared me growing up was being taught how a nation would fall if it stood opposed to Israel. Every time I would see a news broadcast in which the United States military or a politician would not completely support Israel, I was terrified it might be the end of the country or worse. It sounds silly, but imagine being told all your life our safety is contingent on whether or not we agree with the ideologies and cooperation of another country.

TENTH ARTICLE OF FAITH

The tenth Article of Faith states, "We believe in the literal gathering of Israel and in the restoration of the Ten Tribes; that Zion (the New

Jerusalem) will be built upon the American continent; that Christ will reign personally upon the earth; and, that the earth will be renewed and receive its paradisiacal glory." The Mormon Church holds a Postmillennial view. This means they believe there will be an age of peace and prosperity on the earth, after which the coming of Christ will occur at the end of the millennium. Premillennialism on the other hand is the belief Christ will reign before the millennium. Both premillennialism and postmillennialism are not new to the religious world. A man named Cerinthus in A.D. 100 was an early premillennialist who taught Christ would establish a kingdom on earth, centered in Jerusalem, followed by the millennium to be spent in wedding festivities. Since then it has developed into the doctrine Christ will reign on earth upon His second coming. This teaching contradicts what the Bible teaches, but religions such as the LDS Church have still adopted it into their faith system. The tenth Article of Faith mentions a few claims deserving to be dissected.

Will There Be a Literal Gathering of Israel and Restoration of the Ten Tribes?

Context is imperative when examining the land promise given to Israel. Millennialists contend Canaan was unconditionally promised to the descendants of Abraham. They claim since the promise was never completely fulfilled, Abraham must be raised from the dead and the Jews will be restored to their land so the Abrahamic covenant can be fulfilled. However, the Bible describes the land as already having been given to them and the Lord's promise was fulfilled a long time ago.

There were six cities of refuge mentioned in the Bible. Moses writes, "And if the Lord thy God enlarge thy coast, as he hath sworn unto thy fathers, and give thee all the land which he promised to give unto thy fathers; If thou shalt keep all these commandments to do them, which I command thee this day, to love the Lord thy God, and to walk ever in his ways; then shalt thou add three cities more for thee, beside these three:" (Deut. 19:8-9). Joshua also makes clear there were six cities (Josh. 20:7-8). Since there were six cities, it is clear God kept His promise. When David was king, he recovered the land which had been taken by their enemies (2 Sam. 8:1-3). How could David recover something unless it had been possessed and lost?

ESCHATOLOGY

Solomon shows how he reigned over the land promised to Abraham. Moses writes, "On the same day the Lord made a covenant with Abram, saying: "To your descendants I have given this land, from the river of Egypt to the great river, the River Euphrates— the Kenites, the Kenezzites, the Kadmonites, the Hittites, the Perizzites, the Rephaim, the Amorites, the Canaanites, the Girgashites, and the Jebusites" (Gen. 15:18, NKJV). The same is confirmed in 1 Kings 4:21: "And Solomon reigned over all kingdoms from the river unto the land of the Philistines, and unto the border of Egypt: they brought presents, and served Solomon all the days of his life." It is further stated in the book of Second Chronicles: "And he reigned over all the kings from the river even unto the land of the Philistines, and to the border of Egypt" (2 Chron. 9:26). How could Solomon reign over a land which they never possessed?

Moses records the promise by God:

> And I have also established my covenant with them, to give them the land of Canaan, the land of their pilgrimage, wherein they were strangers. And I have also heard the groaning of the children of Israel, whom the Egyptians keep in bondage; and I have remembered my covenant. Wherefore say unto the children of Israel, I am the Lord, and I will bring you out from under the burdens of the Egyptians, and I will rid you out of their bondage, and I will redeem you with a stretched out arm, and with great judgments: And I will take you to me for a people, and I will be to you a God:and ye shall know that I am the Lord your God, which bringeth you out from under the burdens of the Egyptians. And I will bring you in unto the land, concerning the which I did swear to give it to Abraham, to Isaac, and to Jacob; and I will give it you for an heritage:I am the Lord (Exo. 6:4-8)

Joshua confirms how the promise was fulfilled:

> And the Lord gave unto Israel all the land which he sware to give unto their fathers; and they possessed it, and dwelt therein. And the Lord gave them rest round about, according to all that he sware unto their fathers:and there stood not a man of all their enemies before them; the

> Lord delivered all their enemies into their hand. There failed not ought of any good thing which the Lord had spoken unto the house of Israel; all came to pass [emph., NF]" (Josh. 21:43-45)

The promise by God that the land was given to Israel is validated in numerous places in the Bible (1 King. 8:56; Neh. 9:7-8). However, possessing the land was conditional. If they disobeyed God they would lose it. Joshua writes, "When ye have transgressed the covenant of the Lord your God, which he commanded you, and have gone and served other gods, and bowed yourselves to them; then shall the anger of the Lord be kindled against you, and ye shall perish quickly from off the good land which he hath given unto you" (Josh. 3:16). Moses gave the same caution earlier in Deuteronomy 8:19-20 and 30:15-20.

Just as they were warned, the nation of Israel forgot God and were punished. Jeremiah writes, "…Thus saith the LORD of hosts; Even so will I break this people and this city, as one breaketh a potter's vessel, that cannot be made whole again…" (Jer. 19:11) Christ declared the same thing years later to His apostles by way of a parable (Matt. 21:33-43). This was all settled in A.D.70 upon the prophesied destruction of Jerusalem (Matt 24:4-34). A future restoration is not possible because all records, including the Ten Tribes, were destroyed at that time. Ezra said they could not be restored without establishment of descent, family, tribe, and estates.

Millennialists fall short in their alleged prediction since the promise was fulfilled long ago. Whereas the children of Israel lost their land when they were taken captive by Nebuchadnezzar, they came out of captivity and possessed the land. They were restored to the land. This restoration occurred during the reign of Cyrus, King of Persia when he defeated Babylon.

Ezra writes,

> Now in the first year of Cyrus king of Persia, that the word of the Lord by the mouth of Jeremiah might be fulfilled, the Lord stirred up the spirit of Cyrus king of Persia, that he made a proclamation throughout all his kingdom, and put it also in writing, saying, Thus saith

Cyrus king of Persia, The Lord God of heaven hath given me all the kingdoms of the earth; and he hath charged me to build him an house at Jerusalem, which is in Judah. Who is there among you of all his people? his God be with him, and let him go up to Jerusalem, which is in Judah, and build the house of the Lord God of Israel, (he is the God,) which is in Jerusalem (Ezra 1:1-3).

Jeremiah writes,

> And this whole land shall be a desolation, and an astonishment; and these nations shall serve the king of Babylon seventy years. And it shall come to pass, when seventy years are accomplished, that I will punish the king of Babylon, and that nation, saith the Lord, for their iniquity, and the land of the Chaldeans, and will make it perpetual desolations. And I will bring upon that land all my words which I have pronounced against it, even all that is written in this book, which Jeremiah hath prophesied against all the nations (Jer. 25:11-13)

Nehemiah prayed for the children of Israel to be restored according to the promise made by Moses (Neh. 1:8-11). God answered that prayer in Nehemiah's day. Millennialists constantly try to find passages to corroborate their confused theology. They argue Isaiah's prophecy will be fulfilled with the establishment of the "millennial kingdom."

Isaiah writes,

> And it shall come to pass in the last days, that the mountain of the Lord 's house shall be established in the top of the mountains, and shall be exalted above the hills; and all nations shall flow unto it. And many people shall go and say, Come ye, and let us go up to the mountain of the Lord, to the house of the God of Jacob; and he will teach us of his ways, and we will walk in his paths: for out of Zion shall go forth the law, and the word of the Lord from Jerusalem" (Isa. 2:2-3).

Paul clarifies years later the "house" under consideration is Christ's church. He writes, "But if I tarry long, that thou mayest know how thou oughtest to behave thyself in the house of God, which is the church of the living God, the pillar and ground of the truth" (1 Tim. 3:15). Peter spoke of the last days as beginning on Pentecost (Acts 2:16-17). Notice Peter did not say we are in the "next to the last days." The Hebrews writer confirms, "God, who at sundry times and in divers manners spake in time past unto the fathers by the prophets, Hath in these last days spoken unto us by his Son, whom he hath appointed heir of all things, by whom also he made the worlds;" (Heb. 1:1-2)

Millennialists also argue Isaiah's prophecy refers directly to a future kingdom by using Isaiah 11:1-16. However, Daniel identifies the "holy mountain" as the church (Dan. 2:35, 44). Furthermore, Paul quoted Isaiah 11:10 in the New Testament to confirm the reception of the Gentile nations by the church. He writes, "And again, Esaias saith, There shall be a root of Jesse, and he that shall rise to reign over the Gentiles; in him shall the Gentiles trust" (Rom. 15:12).

In order for true restoration to occur, several things would need to take place. First, there would need to be an identification of all tribes. Since all records were lost in the destruction of Jerusalem in A.D. 70, this would be impossible. Second, there would need to be a division of the lands according to the Old Testament. Third, there would need to be a reestablishment of the Levitical priesthood. There would also need to be a return to the method of worship under the Old Testament priesthood. Finally, there would need to be a full restoration of the Law of Moses. Consider all of this would nullify the work of Christ and destroy His gospel system.

Will Zion be Built on the American Continent?

Believing Zion will be reestablished on American soil was exciting for me. I remember thinking how extraordinary it would be to live during a point in time where prophecy could be fulfilled. The belief is connected to the Mormon teaching Christ literally walked on the American continent during His earthly ministry. The Book of Mormon states, "And it came to pass in the thirty and sixth year, the people were

ESCHATOLOGY

all converted unto the Lord, upon all the face of the land, both Nephites and Lamanites, and there were no contentions and disputations among them, and every man did deal justly one with another." (2 Nephi 4:2)

An article on the official LDS website declares,

> The remarkable community of Zion described in 4 Nephi was established on the American continent sometime between the 34th and 36th years after the birth of our Lord. Discipleship in Christ was the foundation of that community. All social progress and goodness centered in Jesus Christ, whose visitation to America after His Resurrection established an age of righteousness lasting about 165 years. Every individual was wholly converted to the Savior—to His ideas and exemplary behavior… (Skinner)

A plaque located at Temple square in Salt Lake City, Utah reads, "During His ministry in the New World [America – NF], Jesus Christ taught the people, "Ye are they of whom I said: Other sheep I have which are not of this fold." (3 Nephi 15:21) It is a teaching incorrectly based on the words of Christ. John writes, "I am the good shepherd, and know my sheep, and am known of mine. As the Father knoweth me, even so know I the Father:and I lay down my life for the sheep. And other sheep I have, which are not of this fold:them also I must bring, and they shall hear my voice; and there shall be one fold, and one shepherd." (Joh 10:14-16). Consider Jesus' audience was the Jews when He made this decree. In other words, He had "other sheep…not of this [Jewish – NF] fold." The only other sheep at that point who were not of the Jewish fold were the Gentiles.

Christ came to set up a universal system for salvation and His assertion was Jews and Gentiles would be united under such. Paul affirms in his letter to the Corinthians, "For by one Spirit are we all baptized into one body, whether we be Jews or Gentiles, whether we be bond or free; and have been all made to drink into one Spirit." (1 Cor 12:13) He further writes, "There is neither Jew nor Greek, there is neither bond nor free, there is neither male nor female:for ye are all one in Christ Jesus. And if ye be Christ's, then are ye Abraham's seed, and heirs according to the promise." (Gal 3:28-29)

Micah prophesies,

> But in the last days it shall come to pass, that the mountain of the house of the Lord shall be established in the top of the mountains, and it shall be exalted above the hills; and people shall flow unto it. And many nations shall come, and say, Come, and let us go up to the mountain of the Lord, and to the house of the God of Jacob; and he will teach us of his ways, and we will walk in his paths: for the law shall go forth of Zion, and the word of the Lord from Jerusalem (Mic 4:1-2)

Jews and Gentiles would become one flock, or one church. There is absolutely no evidence in the Bible or anywhere else supporting the false claim Christ walked on the American continent. In fact, the Mormon Church is the only religious organization to make such a presumption, and certainly to the degree it will even be restored as the "New Jerusalem."

Will Christ Reign Personally Upon the Earth?

Neither the premillennial nor postmillennial teaching Christ will physically walk on the earth upon His second coming can be found in the Bible. Rather, the Bible reveals an opposing description.

Paul writes,

> But I would not have you to be ignorant, brethren, concerning them which are asleep, that ye sorrow not, even as others which have no hope. For if we believe that Jesus died and rose again, even so them also which sleep in Jesus will God bring with him. For this we say unto you by the word of the Lord, that we which are alive and remain unto the coming of the Lord shall not prevent them which are asleep. For the Lord himself shall descend from heaven with a shout, with the voice of the archangel, and with the trump of God: and the dead in Christ shall rise first: Then we which are alive and remain shall be caught up together with them in the clouds, to meet the Lord in the air: and so shall we ever be with the Lord. (1 Thes 4:13-17)

There is not one Bible passage mentioning Christ will set foot on earth. It does state we will meet Him in the air. This will happen "in the twinkling of an eye" (1 Cor 15:52). There is no reason for the Son of God to be on earth. His kingdom was established once and for all (Acts 2), and is a kingdom that will last forever (Dan 2:44). It was a kingdom fulfilling prophecy and is now the hope of eternal glory. Jesus told Peter, "...upon this rock I will build my kingdom" (Mat 16:18). John the Baptist let it be known how soon the kingdom would happen. Matthew writes, "In those days came John the Baptist, preaching in the wilderness of Judaea, And saying, Repent ye:for the kingdom of heaven is at hand." (Matt. 3:1-2)

Some premillennialists claim Jesus thought the kingdom was at hand, but He did not expect to be rejected in such a manner. Paul disagreed. He writes, "Moreover, brethren, I declare unto you the gospel which I preached unto you, which also ye have received, and wherein ye stand; By which also ye are saved, if ye keep in memory what I preached unto you, unless ye have believed in vain. For I delivered unto you first of all that which I also received, how that Christ died for our sins according to the scriptures; And that he was buried, and that he rose again the third day according to the scriptures." (1 Cor. 15:1-4)

Mark writes, "And he said unto them, Verily I say unto you, That there be some of them that stand here, which shall not taste of death, till they have seen the kingdom of God come with power." (Mark 9:1) If the kingdom has not already been established, some of these men would still be alive today. However, an examination of history verifies all apostles are indeed deceased. Paul states when Christ comes, the kingdom will be delivered up to the Father, not established (1 Cor. 15:23-26).

Premillennialism and Postmillennialism implies certain things about Christ that are false. First, it suggests He is not powerful enough to do what He came to do – set up His kingdom. This in turn calls His omnipotence into question. Second, if He was unable to set up His kingdom the first time, what assurance is there He will not fail again? Finally, it implies the church was an after-thought or a stop-gap measure rather than a part of the eternal plan of God (Eph 3:8-11). The thought the Savior is limited like this is not only ludicrous but also profane.

BREAKING THE CHAINS
Will the Earth be "Renewed?"

Numerous religious groups who believe there will be a "new earth" have adopted this concept. However, the Bible once again offers the truth on the subject.

Peter writes, "Whereby the world that then was, being overflowed with water, perished: But the heavens and the earth, which are now, by the same word are kept in store, reserved unto fire against the day of judgment and perdition of ungodly men." (2 Pet 3:6-7) That judgment will come quickly and suddenly.

The apostle continues,

> But the day of the Lord will come as a thief in the night; in the which the heavens shall pass away with a great noise, and the elements shall melt with fervent heat, the earth also and the works that are therein shall be burned up. Seeing then that all these things shall be dissolved, what manner of persons ought ye to be in all holy conversation and godliness, Looking for and hasting unto the coming of the day of God, wherein the heavens being on fire shall be dissolved, and the elements shall melt with fervent heat (2 Pet 3:10-12)

Notice Peter never said there would even be a new refurbished earth for the Lord or anyone else to inhabit. No Biblical writer attests to this because it is simply not true. John writes, "And I saw a new heaven and a new earth:for the first heaven and the first earth were passed away; and there was no more sea. And I John saw the holy city, new Jerusalem, coming down from God out of heaven, prepared as a bride adorned for her husband." (Rev 21:1-2) "Heaven" and "earth" refer to places of existence. John was describing a realm for the saved. Again, there is absolutely no mention of a physical earth. Jesus proclaimed, "Lay not up for yourselves treasures upon earth, where moth and rust doth corrupt, and where thieves break through and steal: But lay up for yourselves treasures in heaven, where neither moth nor rust doth corrupt, and where thieves do not break through nor steal." (Mat 6:19-20) There is no room in His vivid description for a physical earthly paradise.

It was later when I learned how this millennial belief fails for a number of reasons contradicting Bible history. Context is imperative when examining the land promise and Israel. Millennialists contend Canaan was unconditionally promised to the descendants of Abraham. They claim since the promise was never completely fulfilled, Abraham must be raised from the dead and the Jews must be restored to their land so the Abrahamic covenant can be fulfilled. However, the Bible describes the land as already having been given to them and the Lord's promise was fulfilled a long time ago.

WORKS CITED

Skinner, Andrew C. From Zion to Destruction: The Lessons of 4 Nephi. September 2000. 28 October 2014 <http://www.lds.org >.

6

LDS PROPHECIES

Perhaps nothing intrigued me more growing up than studying prophecy. The LDS Church argues many of theirs have been fulfilled. I remember church leaders speak of fulfilled prophecies at General Conference. Teachers would often arrange entire lessons around them. While they held my interest, admittedly they also made me nervous since some hinged on "end times." I wanted to know details and how these supernatural predictions came to pass. Some of my church leaders were exceptional at explaining them in a captivating way to demand my attention. However, the more I looked at many of the prophecies the more I realized how they could be easily explained or utterly failed altogether. I was told repeatedly how those who challenged the accuracy of Mormon prophecies were just spreading propaganda. My problem is I learned to compartmentalize the facts and looked for any element to validate Joseph Smith no matter how inconsequential.

Moses asks a relevant question pertaining to predictive prophecy by writing, "…How shall we know the word which the Lord hath not spoken?" (Deut. 18:21) In other words, how will we know if what someone says is true or false? He then answers it, "When a prophet speaketh in the name of the Lord, if the thing follow not, nor come to pass, that is the thing which the Lord hath not spoken, but the prophet hath spoken it presumptuously: thou shalt not be afraid of him" (Deut. 18:22) In short, if someone gives an accurate prophecy, they may be

87

trusted. If not, then they expose themselves as fraudulent. It only takes one false prophecy to identify a false prophet.

Consider the legitimacy of Bible prophecy. In 1969 a scientist named Peter Stoner wrote an article in the magazine Science Speaks titled "Scientific Proof of the Accuracy of Prophecy and the Bible." He examined the mathematical probability of eight prophecies as recorded in the Old Testament and wrote,

> We find that the chance that any man might have lived down to the present time and fulfilled all eight prophecies is 1 in 10 to the 17th power…take 10 to the 17th power silver dollars and lay them on the face of Texas. They will cover all of the state two feet deep. Now mark one of these silver dollars and stir the whole mass thoroughly, all over the state. Blindfold a man and tell him that he can travel as far as he wishes, but he must pick up one silver dollar and say that this is the right one. What chance would he have of getting the right one? Just the same chance that the prophets would have had of writing these eight prophecies and having them all come true in any one man.

Stoner then considered 48 prophecies and writes, "We find the chance that any one man fulfilled all 48 prophecies to be one in ten to the 157th power…" Those are certainly staggering odds. But ponder there were over two hundred prophecies in the Old Testament that happened exactly when, how, and where the prophet said they would. Every one of them was fulfilled (33 in one day)! No other book of religious antiquity provides such explicit prophecies with precise results. However, it does not take long to see how Mormon prophets have fallen short.

MORMON PROPHECIES THAT HAVE FAILED

Book of Mormon

The Book of Mormon states, "And behold, he shall be born of Mary, at Jerusalem which is the land of our forefathers, she being a virgin, a precious and chosen vessel…" (Alma 7:10) This prophecy can be immediately dismissed as false. John writes, "Hath not the scripture said, That Christ cometh of the seed of David, and out of the town of Bethlehem, where David was?" (Joh. 7:42) Matthew writes, "Now when Jesus was born in Bethlehem of Judaea in the days of Herod the king…" (Matt. 2:1) Likewise, Luke describes the time and setting of the Savior's birth (Luke 2). Jerusalem and Bethlehem are a distance of five miles apart from each other. Geographically they are not the same, nor do they share an immediate neighborhood, as Mormon theologians would have one believe. In order to try to reconcile their false assertions, Mormon apologists claim the "New World" knew little of "Old World" geography. However, notice how John's account clearly refers to geographic details even at the time of David. Micah writes, "But thou, Bethlehem Ephratah, though thou be little among the thousands of Judah, yet out of thee shall he come forth unto me that is to be ruler in Israel; whose goings forth have been from of old, from everlasting." (Mic. 5:2) Throughout Old Testament history there is a distinct difference between Bethlehem and Jerusalem. The only one who seemed to have a problem with "Old World" and "New World" geography was Joseph Smith. This prophecy fails.

Doctrine and Covenants

A prophecy was given regarding where a Mormon temple would be built. Joseph Smith writes,

> Hearken, O ye elders of my church, saith the Lord your God, who have assembled yourselves together, according to my commandments, in this land, which is the land of Missouri, which is the land which I have appointed and consecrated for the gathering of the saints. Wherefore, this is the land of promise, and the place for the city of Zion. And thus saith the Lord your God, if you will receive wisdom here is wisdom. Behold, the place which is now called Independence is the center place; and a spot for the temple is lying westward, upon a lot which is not far from the courthouse (Doctrine & Covenants 57:1-3)

BREAKING THE CHAINS

In other words, there would be a Mormon temple erected in Independence, Missouri. However, to this day there has never been one built nor is there any authorization from the government to establish one. There were temple grounds marked with a cornerstone in 1831, but the members of the LDS Church were forced to flee from Independence in 1833. In 1927 there was a temple started, but was abandoned. This prophecy fails.

There was another prophecy regarding the Civil War. Smith predicts,

> Verily, thus saith the Lord concerning the wars that will shortly come to pass, beginning at the rebellion of South Carolina, which will eventually terminate in the death and misery of many souls; And the time will come that war will be poured out upon all nations, beginning at this place. For behold, the Southern States shall be divided against the Northern States, and the Southern States will call on other nations, even the nation of Great Britain, as it is called, and they shall also call upon other nations, in order to defend themselves against other nations; and then war shall be poured out upon all nations (Doctrine & Covenants 87:1-3)

The Civil War was fought between the North and South, isolated to the United States at that time and never extended beyond the borders of America. It certainly did not pour out upon all nations. Mormon apologists have tried adamantly to ratify this by putting up a smoke screen saying this is not just limited to the Civil War. They have emphasized how "war shall be poured out upon all nations" and not "the war." Interesting how the details prior to and following directly correlate with events having to do exclusively to the United States of America. Then they change it when it did not happen quite like Joseph thought it would. This prophecy fails.

There was a prophecy about David W. Patten, an original member of the Quorum of the Twelve Apostles. Smith wrote, "Verily thus saith the Lord: It is wisdom in my servant David W. Patten, that he settle up all his business as soon as he possibly can, and make a disposition of his merchandise, that he may perform a mission unto me next spring, in company with others, even twelve including himself, to testify of my name and bear glad tidings unto all the world." (Doctrine & Covenants 114:1) This was supposedly a revelation given on April 11, 1838. Patten was killed at the Battle of Crooked River on October 25, 1838 and never made it to the following spring. This prophecy fails.

Additional Failed Prophecies

In Smith's History of the Church, he gives a prophecy pertaining to Lyman E. Johnson, one of their modern day apostles at that time. Smith writes, "…he [Lyman E. Johnson] shall live until the gathering is accomplished, according to the holy prophets; and he shall be like unto Enoch; and his faith shall be like unto his…and he shall see the Saviour come and stand upon the earth with power and great glory." (Smith, History of the Church) Smith claims Johnson would be alive to see the Lord return. This was written in February, 1835. However, Johnson was excommunicated in 1837 and drowned in 1856. This prophecy fails.

Also in History of the Church, Smith has a prophecy about William E. McLellin, another modern day apostle. Smith writes, "…his life shall be spared in the midst of pestilence and destruction, and in the midst of his enemies. He shall be a prince and savior to God's people. The tempter shall not overcome him…and his days may be prolonged until the coming of the Son of Man" (Smith, History of the Church) This was also written in 1835. However, McLellin was excommunicated the same year and died on April 24, 1883. This prophecy fails.

On May 6, 1843 Joseph Smith wrote concerning Judge Stephen A. Douglas,

> I prophecy in the name of the Lord God of Israel, unless the United States redress the wrongs committed upon the Saints in the state of Missouri and punish the crimes committed by her officers that in a few years the government will be utterly overthrown and wasted, and there will not be so much as a potsherd left for their wickedness in permitting the murder of men, women and children, and the wholesale plunder and extermination

of thousands of her citizens to go unpunished, thereby perpetrating a foul and corroding blot upon the fair fame of this great republic, the very thought of which would have caused the high-minded and patriotic framers of the Constitution of the United States to hide their faces with shame. Judge, you will aspire to the presidency of the United States; and if ever you turn uyour hand against me or the Latter-day Saints, you will feel the weight of the hand of Almighty upon you; and you will live to see and know that I have testified the truth to you; for the conversation of this day will stick to you through life. (Smith, History of the Church 394)

The United States Government did not redress any of the wrongs committed against the Mormons in Missouri in 1843. In fact they still stand today over 170 years after this was threatened. This prophecy fails.

Another prophecy concerning government had to do with Congress. Smith wrote, "...I prophesied, by virtue of the holy Priesthood vested in me, and in the name of the Lord Jesus Christ, that, if Congress will not hear our petition and grant us protection, they shall be broken up as a government." (Smith, History of the Church 116) Congress never heard their petition and never granted protection to the Church of Jesus Christ of Latter-day Saints, yet they still function today. This prophecy fails.

There is a prophecy by Joseph Smith regarding inhabitants on the moon.

Oliver B. Huntington wrote,

Astronomers and philosophers have, from time almost immemorial until very recently, asserted that the moon was uninhabited, that it had no atmosphere, etc. But recent discoveries, through the means of powerful telescopes, have given scientists a doubt or two upon the old theory. Nearly all the great discoveries of men in the last half century have, in one way or another, either directly or indirectly, contributed to prove Joseph Smith

> to be a Prophet. As far back as 1837, I know that he said the moon was inhabited by men and women the same as this earth, and that they lived to a greater age than we do – that they live generally to near the age of 1000 years. He described the men as averaging near six feet in height, and dressing quite uniformly in something near the Quaker style. In my Patriarchal blessing, given by the father of Joseph the Prophet, in Kirtland, 1837, I was told that I should preach the gospel before I was 21 years of age; that I should preach the gospel to the inhabitants upon the island of the sea, and – to the inhabitants of the moon, even the planet you can now behold with your eyes. The first two promises have been fulfilled, and the latter may be verified. From the verification of two promises we may reasonably expect the third to be fulfilled also. (Huntington 263-64)

Space exploration was still science fiction, which is precisely what Smith's prediction was. This prophecy fails.

Another prophecy had to do with Smith trying to sell the copyright of the Book of Mormon. At that time, Canada was known to purchase religious material and Smith wanted a part of it.

David Whitmer explains,

> Joseph looked into the hat in which he placed the stone, and received a revelation that some of the brethren should go to Toronto, Canada, and that they would sell the copyright of the Book of Mormon…Well, we were all in great trouble; and we asked Joseph how it was that he had received a revelation from the Lord for some brethren to go to Toronto and sell the copyright, and the brethren had utterly failed in their undertaking. Joseph did not know how it was, so he enquired of the Lord about it, and behold the following revelation came through the stone: "Some revelations are of God: some revelations are of men: and some revelations are of the devil." (Whitmer)

BREAKING THE CHAINS

Consider what convenient reasoning this is, as it implies any false revelation could just be explained away by simply saying it was of the devil or from man. I was constantly told this same thing early in my life. It was an easy way to satisfy me and others who would question different things. No prophecy in the Bible reasons its authenticity in this manner, yet many in defense of Mormon scripture fall for this nonsensical logic. This prophecy fails.

Brigham Young, the second leader of the LDS Church wrote,

> I will tell you who the real fanatics are: they are they who adopt false principles and ideas as facts, and try to establish a superstructure upon a false foundation. They are the fanatics; and however ardent and zealous they may be, they may reason or argue on false premises till doomsday, and the result will be false. If our religion is of this character we want to know it; we would like to find a philosopher who can prove it to us. (Young)

Perhaps if Mr. Young was alive long enough to see this bold proclamation backfire, he would have recanted his confident remarks. Many more failed prophecies can be found with timely research, but it only takes one to correctly expose a false prophet. Several are listed for the sake of identifying the Church of Jesus Christ of Latter Day Saints as being a fallacious religion deceiving many good souls searching for spiritual validation.

MORMON PROPHECIES EASILY EXPLAINED

Some prophecies are not prophecies at all. They are statements masquerading as predictions and attempt to assimilate Bible passages in order to support their intent. Joseph Smith relayed to Sidney Rigdon how the LDS Church would land in the Rocky Mountains and rise to success. Smith wrote, "Zion shall flourish upon the hills and rejoice upon the mountains, and shall be assembled together unto the place which I have appointed." (Doctrine & Covenants 49:25) Several of my teachers explained to me this referred to the Rocky Mountains of Utah and was connected to a fulfillment of Isaiah's prophecy.

Isaiah writes,

> And it shall come to pass in the last days, that the mountain of the LORD'S house shall be established in the top of the mountains, and shall be exalted above the hills; and all nations shall flow unto it. And many people shall go and say, Come ye, and let us go up to the mountain of the LORD, to the house of the God of Jacob; and he will teach us of his ways, and we will walk in his paths: for out of Zion shall go forth the law, and the word of the LORD from Jerusalem. And he shall judge among the nations, and shall rebuke many people: and they shall beat their swords into plowshares, and their spears into pruninghooks: nation shall not lift up sword against nation, neither shall they learn war any more. O house of Jacob, come ye, and let us walk in the light of the LORD. (Isa. 2:2-5)

The problem with their assumption is made clear by Isaiah's own words. Notice he explicitly states the law and the word of the Lord will go forth from Jerusalem. The Lord's house is a reference to the church of Christ and no one or nothing else. Paul writes, But if I tarry long, that thou mayest know how thou oughtest to behave thyself in the house of God, which is the church of the living God, the pillar and ground of the truth." (1 Tim. 3:15) Isaiah saw this happening in the last days, the Christian dispensation. Something big was going to happen at the end of the Jewish dispensation. The mountain is the Lord's house, or church. It is exalted above all nations. It would be a taught nation. It would be permanent in its duration. The Hebrews writer pens, "But ye are come unto mount Sion, and unto the city of the living God, the heavenly Jerusalem, and to an innumerable company of angels, To the general assembly and church of the firstborn, which are written in heaven, and to God the Judge of all, and to the spirits of just men made perfect, And to Jesus the mediator of the new covenant, and to the blood of sprinkling, that speaketh better things than that of Abel." (Heb. 12:22-24)

The Bible distinguishes Zion as the city of David (2 Sam. 5:7; 1 King 8:1; 2 Chron. 5:2). The city of David is recognized as Jerusalem.

BREAKING THE CHAINS

Micah similarly prophesies,

> But in the last days it shall come to pass, that the mountain of the house of the Lord shall be established in the top of the mountains, and it shall be exalted above the hills; and people shall flow unto it, and many nations shall come, and say, Come, and let us go up to the mountain of the Lord, and to the house of the God of Jacob; and he will teach us of his ways, and we will walk in his paths: for the law shall go forth of Zion, and the word of the Lord from Jerusalem. (Mic. 4:1-2)

The LDS Church with their millennial belief is the only religion trying to define Zion as the New Jerusalem and will be set up on the American continent. No Bible passage is in harmony with this error.

One of the key teachings explained to me in Sunday School and Seminary was Ezekiel 37:15-22 predicted the uniting of the Book of Mormon and the Bible with reference to the two sticks and Joseph.

Ezekiel writes,

> The word of the LORD came again unto me, saying, Moreover, thou son of man, take thee one stick, and write upon it, For Judah, and for the children of Israel his companions: then take another stick, and write upon it, For Joseph, the stick of Ephraim, and for all the house of Israel his companions: And join them one to another into one stick; and they shall become one in thine hand. And when the children of thy people shall speak unto thee, saying, Wilt thou not shew us what thou meanest by these? Say unto them, Thus saith the Lord GOD; Behold, I will take the stick of Joseph, which is in the hand of Ephraim, and the tribes of Israel his fellows, and will put them with him, even with the stick of Judah, and make them one stick, and they shall be one in mine hand. And the sticks whereon thou writest shall be in thine hand before their eyes. And say unto them, Thus saith the Lord GOD; Behold, I will take the children of Israel from among the heathen, whither they be gone, and will

gather them on every side, and bring them into their own land: And I will make them one nation in the land upon the mountains of Israel; and one king shall be king to them all: and they shall be no more two nations, neither shall they be divided into two kingdoms any more at all:

Without questioning I was convinced this was a historical prediction and airtight proof of the establishment of the Book of Mormon.

Boyd K. Packer, President of the Quorum of the Twelve Apostles from 2008-2015 wrote,

> In ancient Israel records were written upon tablets of wood or scrolls rolled upon sticks. ... The stick or record of Judah—the Old Testament and the New Testament—and the stick or record of Ephraim—the Book of Mormon, which is another testament of Jesus Christ—are ... indeed one in our hands. Ezekiel's prophecy now stands fulfilled...The older generation has been raised without them, but there is another generation growing up. The revelations will be opened to them as to no other in the history of the world. Into their hands now are placed the sticks of Joseph and of Judah. They will develop a gospel scholarship beyond that which their forebears could achieve. They will have the testimony that Jesus is the Christ and be competent to proclaim Him and to defend Him...I began by quoting Ezekiel, prophet of Judah. Two of those Old Testament verses show ten footnotes. One of the ten leads us to the Book of Mormon, which is another testament of Jesus Christ, where half a world away the prophet Lehi, of the lineage of Joseph, quoted this prophecy: "Wherefore, the fruit of thy loins shall write; and the fruit of the loins of Judah shall write; and that which shall be written by the fruit of thy loins, and also that which shall be written by the fruit of the loins of Judah, shall grow together, unto the confounding of false doctrines and laying down of contentions, and establishing peace among the fruit of thy loins, and bringing them to the knowledge of their fathers in the

latter days, and also to the knowledge of my covenants, saith the Lord." (2 Ne. 3:12.)... One footnote may seem a flimsy thread to tie the two together, but five of the ten footnotes lead us to headings in the Topical Guide where 611 other references broaden our knowledge of this one subject and speak as voices from the dust... Threads are wound into cords that bind together in our hands the sticks of Judah and of Ephraim—testaments of the Lord Jesus Christ...I say again, these references constitute the most comprehensive compilation of scripture information on the mission and teachings of the Lord Jesus Christ that has ever been assembled in the history of the world. (Packer)

This kind of information was powerful to me as a young teenager until I started to investigate Ezra's writing more closely. An examination of the text clearly explains the two sticks refer to Judah and Israel. The two nations would become one. It is a promise relating to the restoration of Israel. It has absolutely nothing to do with Mormon scripture. There is no need to overthink it or try to make it something it is not. There was never a bigger and futuristic meaning as I was told at that time. Connecting this to the Book of Mormon demands a significant amount of creativity and manipulating the context.

One should not merely accept something just because he believes it to be accurate. Christianity is based on evidence. Paul writes of the Bereans, "These were more noble than those in Thessalonica, in that they received the word with all readiness of mind, and searched the scriptures daily, whether those things were so." (Act 17:11).

Most who defend Mormon doctrine are ultimately sincere. However, sincerity does not automatically initiate truth. One who is honest with their research will unveil the facts. It is not to say those who do it will ultimately accept it, but the hope remains all will come to Christ.

WORKS CITED

Ballard, Melvin Joseph. Three Degrees of Glory. Ogden: Zion's Printing and Publishing Co., 1922.

Huntington, Oliver B. "Inhabitants on the Moon." Young Women's Journal (1892): 263-264.

Packer, Boyd K. Scriptures. November 1982. 12 October 2016 <http://www.lds.org/ensign/1982/11/scriptures>.

Smith, Joseph. History of the Church. Vol. 2. Salt Lake City: The Deseret Book Company, 1978. 7 vols.

—. History of the Church. Vol. 2. Salt Lake City: The Deseret Book Company, 1978. 7 vols.

—. History of the Church. Vol. 5. Salt Lake City: Deseret Book Company, 1978. 7 vols.

—. History of the Church. Vol. 6. Salt Lake City: Deseret Book Company, 1978. 7 vols.

unknown, Author. Race and the Priesthood. 20 May 2015 <http://www.lds.org/topics/race-and-the-priesthood>.

Whitmer, David. An Address to All Believers in Christ. Richmond: David Whitmer, 1887.

Young, Brigham. "Intelligence, Etc." Journal of Discourses 7 (1859): 290.

—. "The Gospel - The One-Man Power." Journal of Discourses 13 (1870): 271.

7

THE BOOK OF ABRAHAM AND THE SENSEN PAPYRI

Like many young boys I grew up with a fondness for archaeology, especially after seeing Raiders of the Lost Ark in the movie theatre. What made everything even more captivating was when I learned Joseph Smith obtained a set of ancient scrolls and was even able to decipher their cryptic language and symbols. It was one of the most compelling pieces of LDS antiquity in my mind. I paid close attention when I was told it was part of the Book of Abraham, which was first published in 1842 and later became part of the Pearl of Great Price in 1880. The book is written as a non-Biblical historical account of the patriarch Abraham and claims it clarifies several teachings obscure in the Bible. So many of us were convinced we could enhance our faith based on such a profound account of the most famous of the patriarchal fathers. It is a sensational way to get excited about our history. Joseph Smith claimed to possess an Egyptian papyrus known as the Sensen Papyri. This was meaningful to me since it seemed to provide tangible proof and verify the events in the book were real.

It is noteworthy to point out scholars had only begun translating Egyptian in the early 1820's, the very same decade Smith produced the book of Mormon. As far as I was told, Smith received revelation to make sense of them since he could not interpret Egyptian hieroglyphics. Many LDS apologists still uphold the position today. However, that is not how it reads in the Pearl of Great Price or from other sources.

BREAKING THE CHAINS

The introduction of the book states, "A Translation of some ancient Records, that have fallen into our hands from the catacombs of Egypt. – The writings of Abraham while he was in Egypt, called the Book of Abraham, written by his own hand, upon papyrus."

Later it would unfold Smith actually received the papyri from a traveling showman named Michael Chandler. According to Smith, Chandler received some Egyptian coffins and mummies from his uncle. Smith explains, "On opening the coffins, he discovered that in connection with two of the bodies, was something roled up with the same kind of linen, saturated with the same bitumen, which, when examined, proved to be two rolls of papyrus, previously mentioned. Two or three other small pieces of papyrus, with astronomical calculations, epitaphs, &c., were found with others of the mummies. When Mr. Chandler discovered there was something with the mummies, he supposed or hoped it might be some diamonds or valuable metal, and was no little chagrined when he saw his disappointment." Smith goes on to explain how Chandler was told about him and how he (Smith) possessed some kind of power or gifts to translate. Chandler took his exhibit to Philadelphia where he obtained the certificate of the learned, and then to Kirtland where Smith was living. Smith was confident he could translate it correctly. "Thus I have given a brief history of the manner in which the writings of the fathers, Abraham and Joseph, have been preserved, and how I came in possession of the same – a correct translation of which I shall give in its proper place." (Smith 349-351)

Several key beliefs are contained in the book. It teaches life did not begin at birth, but prior coming to earth.

Smith wrote,

> Now the Lord had shown unto me, Abraham, the intelligences that were organized before the world was; and among all these there were many of the noble and great ones; And God saw these souls that they were good, and he stood in the midst of them, and he said: These I will make my rulers; for he stood among those that were spirits, and he saw that they were good; and he said unto me: Abraham, thou art one of them; thou wast chosen before thou wast born. And there stood one

among them that was like unto God, and he said unto those who were with him: We will go down, for there is space there, and we will take of these materials, and we will make an earth whereon these may dwell; (The Book of Abraham 3:21-24)

Smith also connects this to the belief in many gods, or polytheism. He wrote, "And then the Lord said: Let us go down. And they went down at the beginning, and they, that is the Gods, organized and formed the heavens and the earth." (The Book of Abraham 4:1) This contradicts what the Bible states. John writes, "In the beginning was the Word, and the Word was with God, and the Word was God. The same was in the beginning with God. All things were made by him; and without him was not any thing made that was made." (Joh 1:1-3) Paul agrees, "For by him were all things created, that are in heaven, and that are in earth, visible and invisible, whether they be thrones, or dominions, or principalities, or powers: all things were created by him, and for him: And he is before all things, and by him all things consist." (Col 1:16-17) It was not a multiplicity of gods, but Christ who created all things.

When Joseph Smith died in 1844, the scrolls became property of his wife Emma. She eventually donated them to a museum in Chicago. In 1871, the museum burned as part of the great Chicago fire. It was assumed the papyri were destroyed. However, they were later discovered in the Metropolitan Museum of Art in 1966 and regained attention while becoming public domain. The originals are now located in LDS archives.

I was convinced of Smith's seemingly relevant claim along with everyone I knew. Since it was old and I thought a Prophet was inspired of God to translate it, then I thought surely it had to be true. The apostle Paul writes, "Prove [test] all things..." (1 Thes. 5:21) Perhaps I did not see a need to heed his instruction since what I was taught seemed authentic. As with everything, the truth will eventually rise above what is false.

There are three Facsimiles given attention in the Book of Abraham. Smith provided an explanation of each one. I was smitten with such a find; especially because I was convinced this was yet another piece of evidence ultimately proving Mormon history. I was stunned later upon

BREAKING THE CHAINS

learning their meanings did not match Smith's. Top Egyptologists including Dr. John A. Wilson (professor emeritus of Egyptology at the University of Chicago), Dr. Klaus Baer (associate professor of Egyptology at the University of Chicago's Oriental Institute), and Professor Richard A. Parker (chairman of the department of Egyptology at Brown University) all confirm the papyri as a pagan funerary text known as the Book of Breathings. They are filled with magic and pagan gods, dating a few centuries before Christ. It seems clear Smith had no idea what the papyri actually said. Fortunately, some of the original papyri have been preserved and can be accurately compared to Smith's claims.

Facsimile One

This is how the image appears in the Book of Abraham. Smith numbered various symbols and gave explanations for each one.

He wrote,

Fig. 1. The Angel of the Lord.

Fig. 2. Abraham fastened upon an altar.

Fig. 3. The idolatrous priest of Elkenah attempting to offer up Abraham as a sacrifice.

Fig. 4. The altar for sacrifice by the idolatrous priests, standing before the gods of Elkenah, Libnah, Mahmackrah, Korash, and Pharaoh.

Fig. 5. The idolatrous god of Elkenah.

Fig. 6. The idolatrous god of Libnah.

Fig. 7. The idolatrous god of Mahmackrah.

Fig. 8. The idolatrous god of Korash.

Fig. 9. The idolatrous god of Pharaoh.

Fig. 10. Abraham in Egypt.

Fig. 11. Designed to represent the pillars of heaven, as understood by the Egyptians.

Fig. 12. Raukeeyang, signifying expanse, or the firmament over our heads; but in this case, in relation to this subject, the Egyptians meant it to signify Shaumau, to be high, or the heavens, answering to the Hebrew word, Shaumahyeem.

Here is a picture of the original papyrus from the Book of Breathings:

BREAKING THE CHAINS

Little did I realize how erroneous Smith's descriptions were. Notice how parts of the papyrus are missing. This is significant since it illustrates how Smith manipulated it to his own advantage. Modern Egyptologists have since corrected Smith's descriptions and widely accept the actual translations.

Mathie gives a detailed correction:

> Figure 1 is not the "Angel of the Lord." It is actually the ba which represents the soul of the man who is dead.
>
> Figure 2 is not a depiction of Abraham fastened upon the altar. The figure shown is actually identified as Hor, the same name of the Egyptian god.
>
> Figure 3 is not the idolatrous priest of Elkenah attempting to offer up Abraham as a sacrifice. Notice how the head is missing. The figure is actually Anubis, the god of embalming. He presides over the preparation of the body for embalming, and is always represented as a black figure with the head of a jackal, not a human as Smith conveys.
>
> Figure 4 is not the altar for sacrifice by the idolatrous priests, standing before the gods of Elkenah, Libnah, Mahmackrah, Korash, and Pharaoh. It is actually a "lion couch," or funeral bier. Many scenes like this can be seen in ancient Egyptian art. The context is of death and mummification, not sacrifice as Smith claimed. In fact, human sacrifice was never practiced in Egypt, except maybe in the first dynasty which would have pre-dated Abraham by years. An altar used for human sacrifice would have been unknown at this point.
>
> Figures 5, 6, 7, 8 are not the idolatrous gods of Eklenah, Libnah, Mahmackrah, Korash and Pharaoh. There are no gods ever identified as Elkenah, Libnah, Mahmackrah, or Korash in over 5,000 years of Egyptian history. They are actually canopic jars holding the internal organs of the deceased after embalming. The figures represent the

four sons of the god Horus who are Qebehseneuf, who receives the intestines (Fig. 5), Duamutef, who receives the stomach (Fig. 6), Hapy, who receives the lungs (Fig. 7), and Imsety, who receives the liver (Fig. 8).

Figure 9 is not the idolatrous god of Pharaoh. It actually represents the god Horus.

Figure 10 is not Abraham in Egypt. It is actually a libation platform that bears wines, oils, and a papyrus plant. It is found in almost all drawings of major god figures in Egyptian art and has nothing to do with Abraham.

Figure 11 is not designed to represent the pillars of heaven, as understood by the Egyptians. It is actually the opposite. Egyptians would have seen this as a palace façade, called a "serekh." According to Egyptologist Stephen E. Thompson, it was a frequent decoration. The "serekh" originally depicted the front of a fortified palace.

Figure 12 is not Raukeeang, signifying expanse, or the firmament over our heads, or Shaumau, answering to the Hebrew word, Shaumahyeem. None of those words are Egyptian. Rather, they are Hebrew transliterations. Smith was studying Hebrew with Professor Joshua Seixas at the time he obtained the papyri, and the transliterations are in Seixas's style. (Mathie)

Sandra Tanner explains,

All of the first two rows of characters on the papyrus fragment can be found in the manuscript of the Book of Abraham that is published in Joseph Smith's Egyptian Alphabet and Grammar…A careful examination of the original manuscripts in the handwriting of Joseph Smith's scribes reveals that Smith used less than four lines from this papyrus to make forty-nine verses in the book of Abraham. These forty-nine verses are composed of more than 2,000 English words!…The average number of words that the Egyptologist used to convey the message in this

BREAKING THE CHAINS

text is eighty-seven, whereas Joseph Smith's rendition contains thousands of words. In one Case Joseph Smith derived 177 English words out of the word "Khons" - the name of an Egyptian moon god! (Tanner)

Joseph Smith not only modified the images, but also the descriptions.

Facsimile Two

This is a copy of a hypocephalus, an Egyptian funerary amulet. Smith again offers his descriptions found in Book of Abraham, chapter three:

> Fig. 1. Kolob, signifying the first creation, nearest to the celestial, or the residence of God…

> Fig. 3. Is made to represent God, sitting upon his throne, clothed with power and authority; with a crown

of eternal light upon his head; representing also the grand Key-words of the Holy Priesthood, as revealed to Adam in the Garden of Eden, as also to Seth, Noah, Melchizedek, Abraham, and all to whom the Priesthood was revealed.

Fig. 5. Is called in Egyptian Enish-go-on-dosh; this is one of the governing planets also, and is said by the Egyptians to be the Sun, and to borrow its light from Kolob through the medium of Kae-e-vanrash, which is the grand Key, or, in other words, the governing power, which governs fifteen other fixed planets or stars, as also Floeese or the Moon, the Earth and the Sun in their annual revolutions. This planet receives its power through the medium of Kli-flos-is-es, or Hah-ko-kau-beam, the stars represented by numbers 22 and 23, receiving light from the revolutions of Kolob.

Fig. 7. Represents God sitting upon his throne, revealing through the heavens the grand Key-words of the Priesthood; as, also, the sign of the Holy Ghost unto Abraham, in the form of a dove.

Again, Smith altered this facsimile from the original. Missing portions of the facsimile were copied from other pieces of the papyri purchased by Smith in 1835. Egyptologists offer their expert insight. World renowned Egyptologist Sir Wallis Budge mentioned how Joseph Smith's translation of the amulet had no archaeological value. (Budge)

Figure 1 is not a planet called Kolob, nor does it describe a place near the residence of God. It is actually Knum, a ram-headed god (Fig. 1) between Thoth's baboons (Fig. 22, 23) who have disks on their heads and stand in the posture of adoration.

Figure 3 has been immediately recognized by Egyptologists as the well-known scene of the falcon-headed god Ra (or Re) with a sun disk on his head. "A sun god, Ra is sitting in his solar bark. In Egyptian idolatry, at the end of each day Ra journeys through the underworld in his solar bark along with several other deities.

BREAKING THE CHAINS

Figure 7 does not represent God on his throne or the Holy Ghost standing next to him. The "Holy Ghost" is actually identified as the snake god Nehebkau. "God" is actually Min-Horus. (Hines)

The entire assortment of images comes from a pagan amulet known as a hypocephalus. It would be placed under the head of a mummy. Its magical function was to retain body heat so the soul could reoccupy the body. Again, Hor's name is identified in the translation. It was never found on mummies prior to 660 B.C. which post-dates Abraham, thus dismissing the possibility of Abraham as the author.

Facsimile Three

This final scene can be found in Book of Abraham, chapter five. Smith once offers his explanation:

> Fig. 1. Abraham sitting upon Pharaoh's throne, by the politeness of the king, with a crown upon his head, representing the Priesthood, as emblematical of the grand Presidency in Heaven; with the scepter of justice and judgment in his hand.

Fig. 2. King Pharaoh, whose name is given in the characters above his head.

Fig. 3. Signifies Abraham in Egypt as given also in Figure 10 of Facsimile No. 1.

Fig. 4. Prince of Pharaoh, King of Egypt, as written above the hand.

Fig. 5. Shulem, one of the king's principal waiters, as represented by the characters above his hand.

Fig. 6. Olimlah, a slave belonging to the prine.

Abraham is reasoning upon the principles of Astronomy, in the king's court.

Smith's narrative again differs with the conclusions of numerous renowned Egyptologists:

1. Klaus Baer:

As far as it can be made out, the lines of hieroglyphs below the scene reads:

O gods of . . . , gods of the Caverns, gods of the south, north, west, and east, grant well-being to Osiris Hor, justified. . . .

The characters above and to the left of the man [Figure 5] are probably to be read: "Osiris Hor, justified forever."

(Dialogue: A Journal of Mormon Thought 3 [Autumn 1968]:127)

2. Dee Jay Nelson:

Bottom line [below illustration; This line reads from left to right.]:

"Hail Gods....Cave Gods, Chief of the Hall of the Gods of the south, north, west and east, give vitality to Osiris Hor, who is true of word, (He) makes.....invocations (to thee)." [page 21]

[Another rendition: "Hail Gods....Cave Gods, Chief of the Divine Hall of the south, north, west and east, give vitality to Osiris Hor, who is true of word, (He) makes invocations (to thee)." (page 28)]

To the right of Isis [Figure 2 of Facsimile 3]:

"... Mother of the Gods"

To the right of Osiris [Figure 1 of Facsimile 3]:

"Thou art established, Osiris Hor, in the presence of his great throne."

To the left of Maat [Figure 4 of Facsimile 3]:

Maat; Sayeth Osiris, Chief of Amentt (Western land of the Dead).

In front of the deceased [Figure 5 of Facsimile 3]:

"Osiris Hor, who is true of word (justified) eternally."

In front of Anubis [Figure 6 of Facsimile 3]:

Sayeth Anubis....Lord of Heaven, ...

(A Translation & Study of Facsimile No. 3 In The Book of Abraham [Salt Lake City: Modern Microfilm Co., 1969], 21)

3. Robert K. Ritner:

Label for Osiris (Fig[ure]. 1 of Facsimile 3):

Recitation by Osiris, Foremost of the Westerners, Lord of Abydos(?), the great god forever and ever(?).

Label for Isis (Fig[ure]. 2 of Facsimile 3):

Isis the great, the god's mother.

Label for Maat (Fig[ure]. 4 of Facsimile 3):

Maat, mistress of the gods.

Label for Hor (Fig[ure]. 5 of Facsimile 3):

The Osiris Hor, justified forever.

Label for Anubis (Fig[ure]. 6 of Facsimile 3):

Recitation by Anubis, who makes protection(?), foremost of the embalming booth, ...

Invocation [below illustration; This line reads from left to right.]:

O gods of the necropolis, gods of the caverns, gods of the south, north, west and east, grant salvation to the Osiris Hor, the justified, born by Taikhibiy.

(Dialogue: A Journal of Mormon Thought 33 [Winter 2000], 114-15, [published March 2002]). See also Ritner, "'The Breathing Permit of Hor' Among the Joseph Smith Papyri," Journal of Near Eastern Studies 62 (July 2003):176-77.

4. Michael D. Rhodes:

Bottom line [below illustration; This line reads from left to right.]:

The gods of the West, the gods of the caverns, the gods of the south, north, west, and east say: May Osiris Hor, justified, born of Taykhebyt, prosper.

To the right of Isis [Figure 2 of Facsimile 3]:

The great Isis, mother of the god.

To the right of Osiris [Figure 1 of Facsimile 3]:

Words spoken by Osiris, the Foremost of the Westerners: May you, Osiris Hor, abide at the side of the throne of his greatness.

To the left of Maat [Figure 4 of Facsimile 3]:

Maat, Lady of the West.

In front of the deceased [Figure 5 of Facsimile 3]:

Osiris Hor, the justified forever.

In front of Anubis [Figure 6 of Facsimile 3]:

Words spoken by Anubis who make protection Lord of heaven, Foremost of the Westerners.

(The Hor Book of Breathings: A Translation and Commentary [Provo, Utah: Foundation for Ancient Research and Mormon Studies, Brigham Young University, 2002], 25)

5. Robert K. Ritner:

Concluding Vignette, Col. VIII

(Preserved only as Facsimile 3)

Label for Osiris: (VIII/1) Recitation by Osiris, Foremost of the Westerners, (VIII/2) Lord of Abydos(?), the great god (VIII/3) forever and ever(?).

Label for Isis: (VIII/4) Isis the great, the god's mother.

Label for Maat: (VIII/5) Maat, mistress of the gods.

Label for Hôr: (VIII/6) The Osiris Hôr, (VIII/7) justified forever.

Label for Anubis: (VIII/8) Recitation by Anubis, who makes protection(?), (VIII/9) foremost of the embalming booth(?) (VIII/10) ...

Invocation below scene: (VIII/11) O gods of the necropolis, gods of the caverns, gods of the south, north, west and east, grant salvation to the Osiris Hôr, the justified, born by Taikhibit.

The Joseph Smith Egyptian Papyri: A Complete Edition, Salt Lake City: Smith-Pettit Foundation, 2011, 149, quotation marks omitted) (Ritner)

THE BOOK OF ABRAHAM AND THE SENSEN PAPYRI

It is of interest to emphasize some significant errors. Pharaoh was never described as "polite" or "humble" (Fig. 1). Also, the figure Smith identified as Pharaoh was actually Isis. Further, Abraham is depicted as wearing the otef crown of Osiris (Fig. 1), something he surely would never have done as a stalwart believer in the one God. Finally, the "prince of Pharaoh" (Fig. 4) is actually the female Ma'at as described by the experts. Smith not only assigned the wrong names, but the wrong genders for two of five figures.

In their book Discrimination: Is it of God?, authors Fitzgerald, Nelson and Marqardt confirm all papyrus was related to and written for the same deceased person, Hor, a priest of Amon-Ra at Thebes in Egypt. It is worth mentioning there are at least fifteen Egyptian gods and goddesses were identified on the papyri. At no point was there ever any mention of Abraham, who would have rejected the religious beliefs of the Egyptians.

Additionally, why would an inspired translation from Egyptian to English be so different? Why would the papyri not match the Book of Abraham in the Pearl of Great Price? LDS apologists do their best to explain, but fall short.

> Michael Rhodes, a "researcher in ancient scriptures" at Brigham Young University writes, "One explanation is that it may have been taken from a different portion of the papyrus rolls in Joseph Smith's possession. In other words, we don't have all the papyri Joseph Smith had—and what we do have is obviously not the text of the book of Abraham…A second explanation takes into consideration what Joseph Smith meant by the word translation. While translating the Book of Mormon, he used the Urim and Thummim rather than dictionaries and grammars of the language. Translating with the Urim and Thummim is evidently a much different process than using the tools of scholarly research." (Rhodes)

This is shallow reasoning. First, if it (may have been) taken from a different portion of papyrus rolls and we do not have all of what Smith had, why use it? It is obviously irrelevant and certainly is without any value as evidence. Second, the method of a correct translation, especially if he was inspired, should have no effect on the outcome. There are only two logical conclusions concerning Smith's claims of inspiration. Either the Holy Spirit was factually wrong, or Smith was not inspired. If he was inspired, the Holy Spirit was wrong. If he was not inspired, then the Pearl of Great Price immediately ceases to be divine. It is crucial to reiterate the Pearl of Great Price is "a selection from the revelations, translations, and narrations of Joseph Smith" The inaccuracy of textual facts prove him to be a false teacher just as the errors of the Book of Mormon prove him to be false. This was one of the most difficult concepts to absorb. If I could understand it, why couldn't others?

WORKS CITED

Budge, Wallis. The Mummy, a Handbook of Egyptian Funerary Archaeology. New York: Dover Publications, 1989.

Hines, Mark. Book of Abraham Fraud. 29 April 2015 <http://www.conchisle.com>.

Mathie, Kevin. Examining the Book of Abraham, Chapter 6. 6 May 2015 <http://www.bookofabraham.com>.

Rhodes, Michael. Why Doesn't the Translation of Egyptian Papyri Found in 1967 Match the Text of the Book of Abraham in Pearl of Great Price? 1988. 6 May 2015 <http://www.lds.org/ensign/1988/07/i-have-a-question>.

Ritner, Robert. Breathing Permit of Horus. 29 April 2015 <http://www.user.xmission.com/~research/breathing/index.htm>.

Smith, Joseph. History of the Church. Vol. II. Salt Lake City: The Deseret Book Company, 1978. VII vols.

Tanner, Sandra. Fall of the Book of Abraham. 29 April 2015 <http://www.utlm.org>.

8

THE PLAN OF SALVATION

Along with the confusion about the Godhead, this was the other key subject causing me to leave the LDS Church. Mormonism teaches before this life, everyone has what is called a "Pre-mortal Existence," living and waiting as "spirit children." In other words, before this life everyone lived with the Father in the heavenly realm. The doctrine began to be taught at a very young age. We were asked slanted questions like, "What do you think it was like to live in heaven with Heavenly Father?" "How do you know you chose to follow Jesus in the pre-mortal life?" "What does the fact you chose to follow Jesus in the pre-mortal life tell you about yourself?" We would sing songs about it. Teachers would regularly bear their testimony how we were the spirit children of God.

As a young teenager I remember asking one of my teachers who I trusted about our pre-mortal state. I was curious and wanted to understand our nature before this life. Without referring to the Bible or even mentioning any of the LDS canon, he tried to explain to me we were intelligences and as intelligences we have always existed. This confused me even more, as I had never heard it described like that. It did not make sense to me. We can have intelligence, but how are we intelligence itself? It is still uncertain to me whether he really thought he knew or if he was just trying to answer the question. Either way he was unable to expand on effectively communicating it.

BREAKING THE CHAINS

They teach upon entering this world God provided a plan whereby we can progress to eventually become like Him. For this purpose, He sent us to earth to learn and grow by making right and wrong decisions. They further say when we are sent to earth, God places a "veil of forgetfulness" for us so we cannot remember heaven.

Brigham Young wrote, "It has also been decreed by the Almighty that spirits, upon taking bodies, shall forget all they had known previously, or they could not have a day of trial—could not have an opportunity for proving themselves in darkness and temptation, in unbelief and wickedness, to prove themselves worthy of eternal existence." (Young, Light and Influence of the Spirit, Etc.)

Thomas S. Monson, current President of the Church of Jesus Christ of Latter-day Saints, penned,

> How grateful we should be that a wise Creator fashioned an earth and placed us here, with a veil of forgetfulness on our previous existence, so that we might experience a time of testing, an opportunity to prove ourselves and qualify for all that God has prepared for us to receive. Clearly, one primary purpose of our existence upon the earth is to obtain bodies of flesh and bones. (Monson)

While on earth everyone has the ability to choose. Mormons call this "free agency."

BAPTISM

One of the proudest moments of my life growing up was being baptized into "the Church." Unless one is converted later in life, the standard age to be immersed is eight years old. Every child anxiously awaits it and it is a major event. However, the Mormon Church has a rather different perspective of baptism. While they claim to teach Baptism for the remission of sins, their tradition of what they accept as the age of accountability and why one is baptized and what happens comes with questionable details. The Bishop explained it to me when we turn eight our lives are wiped clean like a white sheet of paper. Everything starts over. From that point angels in heaven are making a list of everything

THE PLAN OF SALVATION

good and everything bad we do. The easiest way to explain it is like a sort of spiritual inventory. Obviously the good must outweigh the bad. Needless to say at that young of an age one can get very nervous about making decisions, especially those who may not be right in the sight of God. Looking back it was a brilliant scare tactic, although they constantly assured us there was nothing with which to fear.

The official LDS website (www.lds.org) states,

> Not long after Moroni was called to be a prophet, disagreements arose in the church about whether little children should be baptized. Moroni wrote a letter to his father, Mormon, asking for advice. Mormon prayed to Heavenly Father and received an answer: "Listen to the words of Christ, your Redeemer, your Lord and your God. Behold, I came into the world not to call the righteous but sinners to repentance; the whole need no physician, but they that are sick; wherefore, little children are whole, for they are not capable of committing sin" (Moroni 8:8). Mormon wrote back to Moroni, telling him, "It is solemn mockery before God, that ye should baptize little children. "Behold I say unto you that this thing shall ye teach—repentance and baptism unto those who are accountable and capable of committing sin. ..."And ... little children need no repentance, neither baptism. Behold, baptism is unto repentance ... unto the remission of sins [emph., NEF]. "But little children are alive in Christ, even from the foundation of the world." (Moroni 8:9–12.) In our own time, the Lord revealed to Joseph Smith that children should be baptized at the age of eight. (See Doctrine and Covenants 68:25, 27 [D&C 68:25, 27]). Each year thousands of righteous children reach the age of accountability and are baptized into the Lord's church. (www.lds.org, "The Age of Accountability: Why Am I Baptized When I am Eight Years Old?")

There are several factors to weigh with these teachings. If children are not capable of committing sin then why the need for baptism? It must be understood Baptism is for the condemned. Baptism for the remission of sins means sin is involved and Baptism washes sin away. Paul writes, "For the wages of sin is death…" (Rom. 6:23). Something must be done to take care of it. Notice how their own doctrine changed and amended the subject. Further, what does it mean by "baptism is unto repentance"? On the Day of Pentecost, when the Jews were pricked in their hearts they asked, "What shall we do?" (Act. 2:37) Peter responded, "Repent, and be baptized every one of you in the name of Jesus Christ for the remission of sins…" (Act. 2:38) Repentance was separate from Baptism and yet of equal importance in order to wash away sins. One cannot receive remission of sins without repenting. One cannot receive remission of sins without baptism. They involve different things. One does not automatically repent upon being baptized, just as one is not automatically baptized upon repenting.

Further, there is nowhere in the Bible confirming the age of accountability is eight years old. Children develop and understand differently from one another. The age of accountability indicates one is fully aware of the decision between doing right and wrong. Scripturally they must demosntrate a recognition of who Christ is. They must realize what repentance is and why it is imperative. They must recognize what will happen if they are not baptized. They must be willing to put God first. Baptism is a commitment. John writes, "Whosoever committeth sin transgresseth also the law:for sin is the transgression of the law." (1 Joh. 3:4) Not every eight year old child is capable of understanding Christ's law. In fact, all I remember on the day I was baptized was how much attention I received. I did not understand the consequences of being burned with fire (Mat 13:40-42), nor was the destroying nature of a sinful state ever explained to me. I had no vivid understanding of what would happen to me if I died before I was baptized and certainly did not comprehend spending eternity in the lake of fire. This is the most important decision anyone will make in this life and they must be at an age mature enough to be able to reason lawlessness in their own life. Where eternity is spent is contingent on repenting, being baptized and knowing why.

The LDS website also states, "Baptism by immersion in water by one having authority is the first saving ordinance of the gospel and is necessary for an individual to become a member of The Church of Jesus Christ of Latter-day Saints and to receive eternal salvation." This is not what Peter taught. The apostle explains, "Then they that gladly received his word were baptized: and the same day there were added unto them about three thousand souls." (Act. 2:41) Peter further states, "…And the Lord added to the church daily such as should be saved." (Act. 2:47). No one can become a member of anything, as it is the Lord who adds them. One may be able to become a member of the Church of Jesus Christ of Latter-day Saints, but if one wants to be part of Christ's church only the Lord can add them based on the commands given by Peter and other apostles.

Mormons also teach "The person who is called of God and has authority from Jesus Christ to baptize, shall go down into the water with the person who has presented himself or herself for baptism…" (Doctrine and Covenants 20:73). However, not one conversion in the Bible attaches this command. If it were the case, baptism would depend on two people and not just one. What if no one had "authority" according to the Mormon definition? Would one's baptism then be invalid? Would one be lost? There is no Biblical account stating one has to have any special authority to baptize another who has confessed Christ and repented and is ready to have their sins washed away.

LIFE AFTER DEATH

After we die, Mormons believe man will enter the Spirit World and go to either Paradise or Spirit Prison. Those in Paradise are the ones who have been baptized and dedicated themselves to the LDS Church. Those who have not lived as a faithful member of the Mormon Church are sent to Spirit Prison. Those in Paradise will have the opportunity to go down to Spirit Prison and minister the LDS gospel to them. They teach there is still an opportunity to respond to the teachings of God even after death because not everyone has heard about the gospel in this life. As a result, everyone will be judged based on his or her works. This is the point at which baptism for the dead is operative.

BAPTISM FOR THE DEAD

The Mormon Church practices a unique ritual called "baptism for the dead" in which one may be baptized on behalf of another who passed away and did not have the opportunity to be baptized in this life. According to the doctrine, some never heard of the gospel of Jesus Christ. Others lived without fully understanding the importance of the ordinance of baptism. Some were baptized but by someone without the proper authority to administer it. Mormonism teaches one must be ordained (deemed worthy) to baptize.

The description on the main web page of the Mormon Church reads,

> Jesus Christ taught that baptism is essential to the salvation of all who have lived on earth (see John 3:5). Many people, however, have died without being baptized. Others were baptized without proper authority. Because God is merciful, He has prepared a way for all people to receive the blessings of baptism. By performing proxy baptisms in behalf of those who have died, Church members offer these blessings to deceased ancestors. Individuals can then choose to accept or reject what has been done in their behalf (www.lds.org).

As a young man in the LDS faith, this was in my mind the most honorable and privileged ritual of which I could participate. My friends and I anticipated the day we would be able to go into the temple and be baptized for those who never had the chance. I considered it a great honor to take part in such a ritual. The process occurs at a large font of water surrounded by twelve oxen (representing the Twelve Tribes of Israel). Through a few interviews with different authorities, I was "ordained" and seen as worthy to participate.

Typically, such as in my case, there was a group going together. It was a big event and one we saw as very spiritual and important for the work of the Church. On the day of the proxy baptisms we arrived at the temple and changed into special white baptismal garments. We were then escorted to the font. We all waited in line patiently and watched as each young man went down into the water where a high-ranking member greeted him to be baptized on behalf of someone deceased. Finally it was my turn. A computer was placed next to the pool with a lengthy list of names on it. These were the individuals who had supposedly passed and possibly waiting for the opportunity to have someone be baptized for them. Mormons are careful to inform when baptism for the dead is performed, those deceased are not being baptized into the Mormon Church against their will. Each person who has left this life still has the right to choose on the other side. Their salvation is still contingent on whether or not they accept and follow Christ while residing in the "spirit world."

I did not know who they were and knew nothing of their background, but still it was uplifting to me. In my mind, I was helping someone get to heaven. I did not count, but would estimate there were close to forty names or so for whom I was being immersed. The man baptizing me would read off each name and dunk me for each one mentioned. They would audibly state they baptize me on behalf of a name on the screen "in the name of the Father, Son and Holy Ghost for the remission of their sins" and immediately submerged me. As soon as they brought me up they went to the next name. It happened quickly and gave me just enough time to catch my breath in between each person named. The whole routine was somewhat repetitive, but the idea was for every name read the person has now been washed clean and can have a chance for the reward of heaven. The number of names read for one getting baptized varies.

Mormons claim this is a fulfillment of Paul's instruction to the Corinthians. Paul writes, "Else what shall they do which are baptized for the dead, if the dead rise not at all? why are they then baptized for the dead?" (1 Cor. 15:29) There are a few things to consider in exegeting this passage. This verse is known as a hapax, which means it is the only reference that can be found in the entire Bible for that particular passage. Upon examination of the entire chapter, it is clear the context is speaking of resurrection and not a proxy baptism. The word "for" (*uper*) is translated with reference to. Notice the middle question: "If the dead rise not at all?" In other words, why should they be baptized for (with reference to) the (resurrection of) dead? If there is no resurrection, what is the point of being baptized?

Joseph Smith wrote,

> ...I give unto you a word in relation to the baptism for your dead. Verily, thus saith the Lord unto you concerning your dead: When any of you are baptized for your dead,

> let there be a recorder, and let him be eye-witness of your baptisms; let him hear with his ears, that he may testify of a truth, saith the Lord; That in all your recordings it may be recorded in heaven; whatsoever you bind on earth, may be bound in heaven; whatsoever you loose on earth, may be loosed in heaven; (Doctrine & Covenants 127:5-7)

Notice how the last part of this mimics what the Savior tells Peter. Jesus says, "And I will give unto thee the keys of the kingdom of heaven: and whatsoever thou shalt bind on earth shall be bound in heaven: and whatsoever thou shalt loose on earth shall be loosed in heaven." (Mat 16:19) Mormonism tries to attach this to a proxy way to salvation. However, it never meant things in this world could be done in order to impact someone else who has already died. The context has to do with the authority granted to the apostles concerning preaching the word of God.

Consider the whole conversation:

> When Jesus came into the coasts of Caesarea Philippi, he asked his disciples, saying, Whom do men say that I the Son of man am? And they said, Some say that thou art John the Baptist: some, Elias; and others, Jeremias, or one of the prophets. He saith unto them, But whom say ye that I am? And Simon Peter answered and said, Thou art the Christ, the Son of the living God. And Jesus answered and said unto him, Blessed art thou, Simon Barjona: for flesh and blood hath not revealed it unto thee, but my Father which is in heaven. And I say also unto thee, That thou art Peter, and upon this rock I will build my church; and the gates of hell shall not prevail against it. And I will give unto thee the keys of the kingdom of heaven: and whatsoever thou shalt bind on earth shall be bound in heaven: and whatsoever thou shalt loose on earth shall be loosed in heaven. Then charged he his disciples that they should tell no man that he was Jesus the Christ. From that time forth began Jesus to shew unto his disciples, how that he must go unto Jerusalem, and suffer many

THE PLAN OF SALVATION

things of the elders and chief priests and scribes, and be killed, and be raised again the third day. (Mat 16:13-21)

Jesus knew His time here was coming to an end. Someone would need to carry on the teaching of His Gospel. He was leaving the authority to the apostles. Baptism for the dead was never even mentioned.

It must be understood who needs to be baptized, and why. Baptism is for the condemned (Mar. 16:16; Rom. 6:23). It is personal for each individual. The one who sins is the one who needs to be baptized in order to take care of it. If the wages of sin is death, something must be done consciously on an individual's part to take care of sin. Baptism is the commandment (Act 2:38; 22:16). The Bible teaches man is responsible for his own sins (Ezek. 18:20). The second LDS Article of Faith states, "We believe that men will be punished for their own sins, and not for Adam's transgression." This alone contradicts a proxy redemption. If men are "punished for their own sins," how could anyone else be able to atone for them? Paul writes, "Wherefore, my beloved, as ye have always obeyed, not as in my presence only, but now much more in my absence, work out your own salvation [emphasis, NF] with fear and trembling" (Phi. 2:12). The inspired writer pens, "And as it is appointed unto men once to die, but after this the judgment" (Heb. 9:27). Death seals a person's fate.

It must also not be overlooked man is held accountable for himself. Each person must hear for himself (Rom. 10:17). Each person must believe/obey for himself (Joh 8:24). Each person must repent of his own sins (Act 2:38). Each person must confess Christ himself (Matt. 10:32-33). None of these can be done on behalf of another. So neither can anyone be baptized for someone else. Jesus made it clear in His account of the rich man and Lazarus their destinations were final. The Savior states, "And beside all this, between us and you there is a great gulf fixed: so that they which would pass from hence to you cannot; neither can they pass to us, that would come from thence" (Luk 16:26). There was not so much as even an implication of someone coming to the rescue of the rich man who had this life to make the necessary preparations for the next.

Jesus affirms,

> When the Son of man shall come in his glory, and all the holy angels with him, then shall he sit upon the

throne of his glory: And before him shall be gathered all nations: and he shall separate them one from another, as a shepherd divideth his sheep from the goats: And he shall set the sheep on his right hand, but the goats on the left (Matt. 25:31-33).

He proclaims, "Marvel not at this: for the hour is coming, in the which all that are in the graves shall hear his voice, And shall come forth; they that have done good, unto the resurrection of life; and they that have done evil, unto the resurrection of damnation" (Joh 5:28-29).

Paul confirms, "For we must all appear before the judgment seat of Christ; that every one may receive the things done in his body, according to that he hath done, whether it be good or bad" (2 Cor. 5:10). It is important for all to realize the decisions made in this life will determine where the next one is served

Joseph Smith wrote,

> Thus came the voice of the Lord unto me, saying: All who have died without a knowledge of this gospel, who would have received it if they had been permitted to tarry, shall be heirs of the celestial kingdom of God; Also all that shall die henceforth without a knowledge of it, who would have received it with all their hearts, shall be heirs of that kingdom; For I, the Lord, will judge all men according to their works, according to the desire of their hearts. And I also beheld that all children who die before they arrive at the years of accountability are saved in the celestial kingdom of heaven. (Doctrine & Covenants 137:7-9)

After the Spirit World comes the Resurrection, followed by the Final Judgment. At this point everyone will be sent to one of four places. There are three kingdoms / degrees of glory along with Outer Darkness. Who will be in each one is contingent on works and desires in this life. The highest is known as the Celestial Kingdom. Next is the Terrestrial Kingdom. Finally there is the Telestial Kingdom. Outer Darkness is reserved for Satan and his followers who have rejected all forms of religion.

THE PLAN OF SALVATION

Mormonism attempts to use the words of Jesus in order to support this claim. John writes, "In my Father's house are many mansions: if it were not so, I would have told you. I go to prepare a place for you." (Joh 14:2) However, note there is absolutely no indication of kingdoms of glory mentioned. The immediate context clarifies when Jesus returns there will be plenty of room in heaven for everyone who is righteous. Christ is speaking to His faithful apostles.

Celestial Kingdom

This is taught as being a realm reserved for those who have kept all commandments and will be in the presence of God the Father and Jesus Christ the Son. This was my goal. I was determined to do everything there was to do in order to attain this kind of glory.

The manual Gospel Fundamentals, published by the LDS Church, reads:

> This is the place where our Father in Heaven and Jesus live. It is a place where people will be happy, and it will be more beautiful than we can imagine. The people who will live in this kingdom will love our Father in Heaven and Jesus and will choose to obey Them. They must have repented of all their sins and must have accepted Jesus as their Savior. They must have been baptized and received the gift of the Holy Ghost. They must have a testimony from the Holy Ghost that Jesus is the Savior.
>
> To live in the highest part of the celestial kingdom is called exaltation* or eternal life. To be able to live in this part of the celestial kingdom, people must have been married in the temple and must have kept the sacred promises they made in the temple. They will receive everything our Father in Heaven has and will become like Him. They will even be able to have spirit children and make new worlds for them to live on, and do all the things our Father in Heaven has done. People who are not married in the temple may live in other parts of the

celestial kingdom, but they will not be exalted. (Church of Jesus Christ of Latter-day Saints)

Within the Celestial Kingdom are three degrees. Joseph Smith claimed he received a revelation telling him in order to be exalted to the highest degree we need to meet certain requirements in addition to righteousness. He wrote, "In the celestial glory there are three heavens or degrees; And in order to obtain the highest, a man must enter into this order of the priesthood [meaning the new and everlasting covenant of marriage]; And if he does not, he cannot obtain it. He may enter into the other, but that is the end of his kingdom; he cannot have an increase." (Doctrine & Covenants 131:1-4) The marriage of which he refers must have its wedding conducted inside of the LDS Temple in a private ceremony.

Terrestrial Kingdom

This is the second degree, or kingdom, of heaven. It is supposedly reserved for those who have rejected Jesus Christ but basically live good and moral lives. In 1832 Joseph Smith and Sidney Rigdon purportedly received a vision.

Smith wrote,

> And again, we saw the terrestrial world, and behold and lo, these are they who are of the terrestrial, whose glory differs from that of the church of the Firstborn who have received the fulness of the Father, even as that of the moon differs from the sun in the firmament. Behold, these are they who died without law; And also they who are the spirits of men kept in prison, whom the Son visited, and preached the gospel unto them, that they might be judged according to men in the flesh; Who received not the testimony of Jesus in the flesh, but afterwards received it. These are they who are honorable men of the earth, who were blinded by the craftiness of men. These are they who receive of his glory, but not of his fulness. These are they who receive of the presence of the Son, but not of the fulness of the Father. Wherefore,

THE PLAN OF SALVATION

> they are bodies terrestrial, and not bodies celestial, and differ in glory as the moon differs from the sun. These are they who are not valiant in the testimony of Jesus; wherefore, they obtain not the crown over the kingdom of our God. And now this is the end of the vision which we saw of the terrestrial, that the Lord commanded us to write while we were yet in the Spirit. (Doctrine & Covenants 76:71-80)

Gospel Fundamentals reads:

> This kingdom is not as wonderful as the celestial kingdom. Even though Jesus will visit the terrestrial kingdom, those who live there will not live with our Father in Heaven, and they will not have all He has. Those who go to the terrestrial kingdom will be honorable people. Some of them will be members of the Church, and others will not. They will be those who did not accept Jesus on earth but later accepted Him in the spirit world. The people who will live there will not be part of an eternal family but will live separately, without families. Our Father in Heaven will give these people the happiness they are prepared to receive.

Telestial Kingdom

This is the third and lowest degree of the afterlife, although one can still enjoy the benefits of having some sort of glory.

Smith claims in his vision,

> ...we saw the glory of the telestial, which glory is that of the lesser, even as the glory of the stars differs from that of the glory of the moon in the firmament. These are they who received not the gospel of Christ, neither the testimony of Jesus. These are they who deny not the Holy Spirit. These are they who are thrust down to hell. These are they who shall not be redeemed from the devil until the last resurrection, until the Lord, even

Christ the Lamb, shall have finished his work. These are they who receive not of his fulness in the eternal world, but of the Holy Spirit through the ministration of the terrestrial; And the terrestrial through the ministration of the celestial. And also the telestial receive it of the administering of angels who are appointed to minister for them, or who are appointed to be ministering spirits for them; for they shall be heirs of salvation. And thus we saw, in the heavenly vision, the glory of the telestial, which surpasses all understanding; And no man knows it except him to whom God has revealed it. (Doctrine & Covenants 76:81-90)

Gospel Fundamentals affirms:

> This kingdom is not as wonderful as the celestial kingdom or the terrestrial kingdom. Neither our Father in Heaven nor Jesus will visit those who live here. Angels will visit these people, and they will have the influence of the Holy Ghost. The people who live in the telestial kingdom are those who did not accept either the gospel or a testimony of Jesus, either on earth or in the spirit world. They will suffer for their own sins in spirit prison until after the Millennium. Then they will finally be resurrected.
>
> While on this earth, they were liars, thieves, murderers, false prophets, adulterers, and those who ridiculed sacred things. They were the people who accepted the beliefs of the world rather than the teachings of Jesus. Many people will live in this kingdom. Our Father in Heaven will give these people the happiness they are prepared to receive.

Notice those who inhabit the Telesial Kingdom are the ones who willfully reject the Gospel of Christ. They are also "These are they who are liars, and sorcerers, and adulterers, and whoremongers, and whosoever loves and makes a lie." (Doctrine & Covenants 76:103) Though they lived these kinds of lives, they at the end accepted the

Most of my peers, teachers, friends, family and me at an early age echoed the sentiments of George Q. Cannon, a member of the early

Quorum of the Twelve Apostles.

Cannon wrote,

> I think it is of great importance to us as a people to know what we shall do. Are we content to aim for telestial glory? I never heard a prayer offered, especially in the family circle, in which the family does not beseech God to give them celestial glory. Telestial glory is not in their thoughts. Terrestrial glory may be all right for honorable Gentiles, who have not faith enough to believe the Gospel and who do right according to the best knowledge they have; but celestial glory is our aim—I perhaps should not say it is the aim, for sometimes it is not, but it is the hope. If into a family that had just offered prayer, and had asked God to lead them into the celestial kingdom, an angel should enter and should say to them that their prayers were useless and that they would never attain unto celestial glory, what a feeling would be produced in the breasts of that family! How sorrowful and afflicted they would feel! Yet, as I have said, while it is the aim of many, they do not act as if it were their true aim. They either misconceive the nature of the duties they have to perform to attain to celestial glory, or else they are very blind indeed. I ask again, what is your aim, or my aim? What do I desire? If I desire celestial glory, the highest law that God has revealed I will be willing to obey, and to observe every word that proceedeth from His mouth. I do not want to speak of myself, but if there is a law that God has revealed and it is necessary to be obeyed before celestial glory can be reached, I want to know it and obey it. All that I am on this earth for is to get celestial glory" (Cannon)

Outer Darkness

According to Gospel Fundamentals, "Outer darkness is where Satan and those who have followed him will live. These people will be those who chose to live with Satan. They will not be forgiven. These people will live forever in darkness, sorrow, and suffering with Satan and the spirits who followed him."

This is a far cry from what the Bible teaches. Jesus emphatically states, "Not every one that saith unto me, Lord, Lord, shall enter into the kingdom of heaven; but he that doeth the will of my Father which is in heaven." (Matt. 7:21) The Savior warns the church of Ephesus, "Remember therefore from whence thou art fallen, and repent, and do the first works; or else I will come unto thee quickly, and will remove thy candlestick out of his place, except thou repent." (Rev. 2:5) On the Day of Pentecost, when the Jews were pricked in their hearts they asked, "What should we do?" Peter answered, "Repent, and be baptized every one of you in the name of Jesus Christ for the remission of sins…" (Act 2:38) Without remission of sins, there is death instead of life (Rom. 6:23). In order to receive the remission of sins one must repent and be baptized in the name of Jesus Christ. A person who refuses to accept the gospel of Jesus Christ would never be baptized in the name of Him. Suggesting their glories of heaven not only contradict what the Bible says, their descriptions violate what Christ has already commanded and will send someone to a sinner's condemnation.

Man Can Become a God

Not only does Mormonism teach Elohim was a mortal who became a god, but man can become one as well if he remains faithful to LDS doctrine. Smith has convinced many, including me at one point, that upon reaching the highest degree of the Celestial Kingdom we can be deity. He explained, "They are they who are the church of the Firstborn. They are they into whose hands the Father has given all things—They are they who are priests and kings, who have received of his fulness, and of his glory; And are priests of the Most High, after the order of Melchizedek, which was after the order of Enoch, which was after the order of the Only Begotten Son. Wherefore, as it is written, they are gods, even the sons of God" (Doctrine & Covenants 76:54-58)

He further writes,

> And again, verily I say unto you, if a man marry a wife by my word, which is my law, and by the new and

everlasting covenant, and it is sealed unto them by the Holy Spirit of promise, by him who is anointed, unto whom I have appointed this power and the keys of this priesthood; and it shall be said unto them—Ye shall come forth in the first resurrection; and if it be after the first resurrection, in the next resurrection; and shall inherit thrones, kingdoms, principalities, and powers, dominions, all heights and depths—then shall it be written in the Lamb's Book of Life, that he shall commit no murder whereby to shed innocent blood, and if ye abide in my covenant, and commit no murder whereby to shed innocent blood, it shall be done unto them in all things whatsoever my servant hath put upon them, in time, and through all eternity; and shall be of full force when they are out of the world; and they shall pass by the angels, and the gods, which are set there, to their exaltation and glory in all things, as hath been sealed upon their heads, which glory shall be a fulness and a continuation of the seeds forever and ever. Then shall they be gods, because they have no end; therefore shall they be from everlasting to everlasting, because they continue; then shall they be above all, because all things are subject unto them. Then shall they be gods, because they have all power, and the angels are subject unto them. (Doctrine & Covenants 132:19-20)

Joseph Smith contended,

> Here, then, is eternal life—to know the only wise and true God; and you have got to learn how to be Gods yourselves, and to be kings and priests to God, the same as all Gods have done before you, namely, by going from one small degree1 to another, and from a small capacity to a great one; from grace to grace, from exaltation to exaltation, until you attain to the resurrection of the dead, and are able to dwell in everlasting burnings, and to sit in glory, as do those who sit enthroned in everlasting power. (Smith 346-47)

BREAKING THE CHAINS

Lorenzo Snow, the fifth President of the LDS Church, coined the phrase, "As God is, man once was. As God is, man may become."

Brigham Young stated,

> The Lord created you and me for the purpose of becoming Gods like Himself; when we have been proved in our present capacity, and been faithful with all things He puts into our possession. We are created, we are born for the express purpose of growing up from the low estate of manhood, to become Gods like unto our Father in heaven. That is the truth about it, just as it is. The Lord has organized mankind for the express purpose of increasing in that intelligence and truth, which is with God, until he is capable of creating worlds on worlds, and becoming Gods, even the sons of God. How many will become thus privileged? Those who honor the Father and the Son; those who receive the Holy Ghost, and magnify their calling, and are found pure and holy; they shall be crowned in the presence of the Father and the Son. (Young 93-94)

How eager I was to make it to this state. I was determined to eventually have power and authority and create my own worlds. Imagine a young man being told he could have abilities greater than any super hero. Obtaining the glory of the Celestial Kingdom seems attractive to anyone seeking prestige or a sense of purpose. However, it contradicts the eternity the Bible describes.

Jesus answered an inquiry from the Sadducees regarding death and marriage by saying man will become like the angels in heaven (Matt. 22:29-30). Mormons take several key passages of the Bible out of context in trying to accommodate their false premise. One such article on their website suggests regarding John 10:33-34, "New Testament passages also point to this doctrine. When Jesus was accused of blasphemy on the grounds that "thou, being a man, makest thyself God," He responded, echoing Psalms, "Is it not written in your law, I said, Ye are gods?" It is necessary to recognize the passage Jesus was referring to in order to understand the context of His statement. Jesus was not merely echoing Psalms but in fact was alluding to the perspective of the

Psalmist. The writer of the particular psalm (Psa. 82) was Asaph, who was rebuking Israel's corrupt judges that were oppressing the people. He was reminding them they would be judged themselves. The word "gods" in that setting referred to judges and magistrates, not deity. Jesus was using the same term in speaking to the Jews who were about to stone Him in their judgment.

The Bible never gives man the same authority as God. On the contrary, he will succumb to the Almighty (Rev. 4). Many in the Mormon Church will believe any Scripture Joseph Smith claims to have interpreted without testing its viability. As I grew I realized not only could I not find becoming a god in the Bible, but it was a self serving and egocentric principle.

The Lord's scheme of redemption as revealed in the Bible clearly differs with what is taught in Mormon theology. There is absolutely no confirmation in the Bible any of the kingdoms of glory are accurate. It is a belief enforced and supported by the LDS Church and the LDS Church only. Christ, on the other hand, confirms what and how everything will occur.

Matthew writes,

> When the Son of man shall come in his glory, and all the holy angels with him, then shall he sit upon the throne of his glory: And before him shall be gathered all nations:and he shall separate them one from another, as a shepherd divideth his sheep from the goats: And he shall set the sheep on his right hand, but the goats on the left. Then shall the King say unto them on his right hand, Come, ye blessed of my Father, inherit the kingdom prepared for you from the foundation of the world:...Then shall he say also unto them on the left hand, Depart from me, ye cursed, into everlasting fire, prepared for the devil and his angels...And these shall go away into everlasting punishment: but the righteous into life eternal (Matt. 25:31-34, 41, 46)

Christ makes it clear there is only one singular kingdom, not three kingdoms as the Mormon Church teach in error. There will not be a separation of glory, other than those who are righteous and unrighteous. Again, I could not just ignore such pronounced evidence. It is imperative to understand the nature and character of God by what He has revealed in the Bible in order for anything else to be of value.

WORKS CITED

Cannon, George Q. "LDS General Conference." Conference Report. unknown, 1900. 55-56.

Church of Jesus Christ of Latter-day Saints. "Gospel Fundamentals." 1992, 2002. The Church of Jesus Christ of Latter-day Saints. 24 August 2016 <http://www.lds.org>.

—. "Gospel Fundamentals." 1992, 2002. The Church of Jesus Christ of Latter-day Saints. 24 August 2016 <http://www.lds.org>.

Monson, Thomas S. "Invitation to Exaltation." June 1993. Church of Jesus Christ of Latter-day Saints. 14 September 2016 <http://www.lds.org/ensign/1993/06/invitation-to-exaltation>.

Smith, Joseph. Teachings of the Prophet Joseph Smith. Salt Lake City: Deseret Book Company, 1938.

Young, Brigham. "Light and Influence of the Spirit, Etc." 19 June 1859. Journal of Discourses. 14 September 2016 <http://www.jod.mrm.org/6/330>.

—. "The Gospel of Salvation, Etc." Journal of Discourses 3 (1852): 93-94.

AFTERWARD

Perhaps the greatest gift the Lord makes available to us is His revealed will. From a literary and historical standpoint the Bible is proven to be worthy as the inspired standard of authority. Paul assures, "For God is not the author of confusion…" (1 Cor. 14:33). By the apostle's own admission he clarifies how the Gospel will not contradict itself. The more I considered this the more I realized I could trust it which led to the changes I had to make. I also understood if I felt this way, there had to be others feeling the same which is why I spent the time I did putting this book together.

The Hebrews writer states, "For the word of God is living and powerful, and sharper than any two-edged sword, piercing even to the division of soul and spirit, and of joints and marrow, and is a discerner of the thoughts and intents of the heart." (Heb. 4:12) This is why the Bible can be trusted. It has been resilient through time, having withstood multiple attempts to destroy its credibility. This also places a responsibility on the reader to study it and weigh the evidence so we do not complicate the message.

One of the main objectives I had to overcome was feelings do not determine truth. This can be the most difficult part of examining what is right because we are creatures of emotion. But feelings can be deceptive. Solomon writes, "There is a way that seems right to a man, but its end is the way of death." (Prov. 14:12) Later he writes, "He that trusteth his own heart is a fool; but whoso walketh wisely shall be delivered." (Prov. 28:26) Having a burning feeling inside, no matter how strong it may be, is the wrong answer if it is not what the Bible says. It took me some time to realize that, but it was necessary. The psalmist writes, "For the word of the LORD is right; and all his works are done in truth." (Psa. 33:4).

Additionally we cannot go beyond what is revealed in the Bible. When we apply what is not there it helps no one. Peter writes, "If anyone speaks, let him speak as the oracles of God…" (1 Pet. 4:11). The word oracle means revelation. In other words, we only have authority to teach what God has revealed. They did not have the Book of Mormon, Doctrine and Covenants, or Pearl of Great Price. I cannot go by what I think or feel.

My desire for those seeking the truth no matter what their background may be is to investigate and hold on to the truth when you find it. I am not the only one who has questioned my faith and beliefs. I am not the only one who has felt deceived or angry or confused. Know you are not alone. It took me a long time before I could find that place where I could write without getting frustrated. Several years after I left the LDS Church I met someone in the church of Christ. I had no idea what to expect, but it changed my life. He gave me the most sound advice anyone could give. He told me to read the book of Acts. It was eye opening. Upon reading it I realized the imperativeness of confessing, repenting, and being baptized so to be added to the only church truly established by Christ (Acts 2). There is hope. I finally found that good place, and I hope you do as well.

Made in the USA
Thornton, CO
05/18/24 22:50:57

c04dcee6-9b17-4563-a7d5-3a541c9a3427R01